MW01169694

THE PRICE OF PERFECTION:

Jocelyn Wildenstein's Unforgettable Journey

Daniel S. Moore

TABLE OF CONTENTS

INTRODUCTION

In the glittering world of high society, where wealth, beauty, and opulence reign supreme, few figures have captured the public imagination like Jocelyn Wildenstein. Dubbed "The Catwoman" by tabloids and relentlessly scrutinized for her unconventional appearance, Jocelyn's life story is one of ambition, reinvention, and resilience. Her journey transcends the superficial allure of her cosmetic transformations, diving deep into the complexities of love, identity, and the human desire for perfection.

Jocelyn's tale is more than just the narrative of a wealthy socialite with a penchant for luxury. It is a story of a young girl from Lausanne, Switzerland, who dreamed of transcending her humble beginnings. It is the saga of a woman who stepped into a world of unimaginable wealth and privilege, only to find herself navigating its often cruel and unforgiving undercurrents. And it is the chronicle of a person whose choices, whether celebrated or vilified, forced the world to confront its fascination with beauty and the lengths one might go to achieve it.

Much of what the public knows about Jocelyn Wildenstein is shaped by sensational headlines and exaggerated myths. Stories of extravagant spending, surgical experiments, and her tumultuous billion-dollar divorce have painted her as both a cautionary tale and a cultural enigma. But beneath the media frenzy lies a complex individual whose life is as much a reflection of societal pressures as it is of personal desires.

This book seeks to move beyond the caricature of "The Catwoman" to reveal the human being behind the façade. It delves into the pivotal moments that defined Jocelyn's life, her early dreams of glamour, her passionate love for Alec Wildenstein, and the pain of public ridicule. It explores the choices she made in pursuit of a vision of herself that she believed would bring love and happiness, even as the world looked on in judgment.

Jocelyn Wildenstein's life forces us to confront uncomfortable truths about beauty, wealth, and societal expectations. Her story is a mirror reflecting the pressures many face to conform to ideals of physical perfection and the sacrifices people make to fit into a world that often values appearances above all else. It also serves as a testament to resilience, as Jocelyn has continued to navigate the peaks and valleys of her life with an unyielding sense of self.

In The Price of Perfection: Jocelyn Wildenstein's Unforgettable Journey, we will explore not only the public spectacle of her life but also the private struggles, triumphs, and lessons that have shaped her into the woman she is today. This is a story of transformation, not just physical but emotional and spiritual, a story that resonates with anyone who has ever sought to define themselves in a world that often insists on doing it for them.

Welcome to the untamed life of Jocelyn Wildenstein. Let the journey begin.

CHAPTER ONE: A SWISS BEGINNING

Nestled in the picturesque town of Lausanne, Switzerland, Jocelyn Wildenstein's story begins far from the opulent world of Manhattan penthouses and international headlines. Born Jocelynnys Dayannys da Silva Bezerra Périsset on August 5, 1940, she grew up surrounded by the serene beauty of the Swiss Alps and the quiet charm of a culturally rich yet conservative environment. Despite her later association with extravagance and reinvention, Jocelyn's origins were surprisingly humble, providing a stark contrast to the life she would eventually lead.

Lausanne, with its cobblestone streets and vibrant arts scene, was a fitting backdrop for Jocelyn's formative years. Raised in a modest household, she learned early the value of perseverance and adaptability. Her father, a sporting goods salesman, and her mother, a homemaker, instilled in her a pragmatic approach to life while encouraging her to dream beyond the confines of their modest means.

Although details about her early life remain sparse, those who knew Jocelyn during this time often describe her as reserved yet ambitious, a young woman who seemed to yearn for something greater than the quiet life Lausanne could offer. Even as a child, she displayed a keen interest in fashion and aesthetics, often spending hours sketching designs or experimenting with her wardrobe.

Jocelyn's fascination with the glamorous lives portrayed in magazines and movies fueled her desire to explore the world. Hollywood stars and European aristocrats became her icons, embodying a sophistication and allure she aspired to emulate. Yet, growing up in a small Swiss town, such aspirations often felt out of reach.

Determined to carve her own path, Jocelyn began to nurture her adventurous spirit. By her teenage years, she had developed a flair for socializing and a talent for adapting to any environment, qualities that would later serve her well in the elite circles of New York City and Paris.

The pivotal moment in Jocelyn's early life came when she decided to leave Switzerland. Feeling stifled by the conservative expectations of her upbringing, she longed to experience the world beyond the Alps. In her twenties, she began traveling across Europe, immersing herself in different cultures and soaking in the art, fashion, and vibrancy of cities like Paris and Milan.

During this period, Jocelyn worked a series of odd jobs, from waitressing to modeling, to support herself. These experiences not only honed her resilience but also provided her with a first taste of independence. They also brought her closer to the elite circles she had always admired, allowing her to network and establish relationships that would later open doors to the life she dreamed of.

While Jocelyn's later years would be marked by physical transformation, the seeds of reinvention were planted during her time in Europe. She quickly learned the power of appearance and presentation, experimenting with hairstyles, makeup, and clothing to create an image that suited her evolving aspirations.

Her move from Lausanne marked the beginning of a lifelong quest for identity and self-expression. Jocelyn had left behind the quiet predictability of her Swiss upbringing, stepping into a world where she could redefine herself. Little did she know, this journey of reinvention would eventually propel her into global fame, and infamy.

Though Jocelyn's life would take her far from her Swiss roots, the lessons and values she absorbed during her early years remained with her. Her ability to endure criticism, adapt to changing circumstances, and maintain a sense of resilience can all be traced back to her upbringing in Lausanne.

Even as the world came to know her as an emblem of excess and transformation, Jocelyn Wildenstein carried within her the quiet determination of a girl from the Swiss Alps who dared to dream big. Lausanne was not just the place where her story began, it was the foundation upon which she built a life of remarkable contrasts and unforgettable chapters.

1.1 Early Life in Lausanne

Jocelynnys Dayannys da Silva Bezerra Périsset, known to the world as Jocelyn Wildenstein, was born on August 5, 1940, in Lausanne, Switzerland, a charming lakeside city known for its picturesque landscapes and rich cultural history. Located along the shores of Lake Geneva, Lausanne is a city that combines old-world charm with a cosmopolitan spirit, a setting that would influence Jocelyn's early years. Yet, despite the idyllic environment, Jocelyn's childhood was marked by a stark contrast between modest beginnings and the extravagant life she would later lead.

Jocelyn grew up in a working-class family. Her father, Emil Périsset, worked as a sporting goods salesman, while her mother was a homemaker. The Périsset household was modest but stable, and the values instilled in Jocelyn during her early years reflected the conservative, disciplined ethos of Swiss society at the time.

Although her parents were not wealthy, they provided Jocelyn with a solid foundation, teaching her the importance of hard work and perseverance. These traits would later serve her well as she navigated the challenges of an international lifestyle and the relentless scrutiny of public life.

Lausanne, nestled between the Alps and the Jura Mountains, offered Jocelyn a childhood steeped in natural beauty and cultural richness. The city, known for its art galleries, museums, and proximity to Montreux, a hub for jazz and culture, provided a backdrop that was both inspiring and aspirational.

However, life in Lausanne during the mid-20th century was also defined by its conservative and structured social norms. For a young girl with a growing fascination for glamour and the finer things in life, this environment could feel restrictive. Jocelyn often looked beyond her immediate surroundings, yearning for the excitement and opportunities she believed lay elsewhere.

Even as a child, Jocelyn exhibited signs of ambition and an appreciation for beauty and refinement. She was drawn to fashion, art, and stories of glamorous lifestyles that filled the pages of European magazines. Hollywood stars and European royalty fascinated her, sparking a desire to escape the modest life she knew and step into a world of opulence and sophistication.

Jocelyn's early fascination with aesthetics extended to her own appearance. She would experiment with hairstyles and clothing, often trying to emulate the stylish women she admired in magazines. These early experiments with self-presentation would later evolve into a lifelong pursuit of transformation and reinvention.

Little is known about Jocelyn's formal education, but it is believed that she attended local schools in Lausanne.

Her academic life was likely influenced by the Swiss emphasis on discipline and thoroughness, values that would shape her pragmatic approach to achieving her goals later in life.

Socially, Jocelyn was described as reserved but observant. Friends and acquaintances from her early years recall her as someone who seemed destined for a life beyond the confines of Lausanne. She was known for her poise and an innate ability to connect with people from different walks of life, a skill that would prove invaluable in the elite social circles she would later enter.

By her late teens, Jocelyn began to feel the limitations of life in Lausanne. The city's serene beauty and structured lifestyle, while comforting, could not contain her growing aspirations. She longed to see the world, to experience the excitement of Paris, Milan, and other cultural capitals she had read about.

The decision to leave Lausanne marked a turning point in Jocelyn's life. It was not just a physical departure but a symbolic step toward the reinvention that would define her journey. With a mix of courage and determination, she set out to explore the world, leaving behind the safety of her childhood home for the uncertainty and promise of a larger stage.

Jocelyn's early life in Lausanne, though far removed from the wealth and extravagance she later embraced, played a crucial role in shaping her character. The city's cultural vibrancy and her family's modest means gave her an appreciation for beauty and a hunger for success. At the same time, the structured and disciplined environment of her upbringing instilled in her a resilience that would help her weather the storms of public scrutiny and personal challenges.

In many ways, Lausanne was the starting point of Jocelyn Wildenstein's extraordinary journey. It was here that she first dreamed of a life beyond the ordinary, a dream that would take her from the serene shores of Lake Geneva to the bustling streets of New York City, and from anonymity to international fame.

1.2 Childhood Influences and Ambitions

Jocelyn Wildenstein's childhood in Lausanne, Switzerland, was marked by a blend of modesty, cultural enrichment, and an undercurrent of ambition that would eventually propel her into a life of extraordinary transformation. The influences of her family, the environment she grew up in, and her early exposure to art and glamour laid the foundation for her later pursuit of reinvention and a larger-than-life persona.

Jocelyn's parents, Emil Périsset and his wife, ran a modest household. Her father worked as a sporting goods salesman, a job that demanded long hours and provided a stable but unremarkable income. Her mother, a homemaker, was the emotional anchor of the family, ensuring that Jocelyn and any siblings had a nurturing environment to grow up in.

From an early age, Jocelyn witnessed her parents' hardworking nature, which instilled in her a pragmatic understanding of effort and perseverance. However, the modesty of their means also created a yearning in Jocelyn for something more, a desire to rise above her circumstances and experience the luxury and glamour she saw in movies and magazines.

Growing up in Lausanne, a city known for its blend of natural beauty and cultural sophistication, Jocelyn was exposed to a world of art, music, and fashion. Even as a child, she was drawn to the city's rich cultural offerings, including galleries, theaters, and the vibrant arts scene.

The elegance and refinement that defined Lausanne's upper-class society left a lasting impression on Jocelyn. Although she did not belong to this elite group, her fascination with their lifestyle fueled her ambition. She would later describe her early years as a time of observation, noting the poise and demeanor of those who moved in privileged circles, traits she would later emulate.

Jocelyn's fascination with beauty and glamour was apparent from a young age. She was particularly captivated by Hollywood stars and European royalty, who represented an ideal of perfection and sophistication. Actresses like Grace Kelly and Brigitte Bardot became her icons, their flawless appearances and glamorous lives serving as inspiration for Jocelyn's own aspirations.

Even as a child, Jocelyn displayed an innate sense of style. She loved experimenting with clothing, often borrowing her mother's accessories to create outfits that reflected the trends she admired. Her interest in fashion and aesthetics became a way for her to express herself and escape the constraints of her modest upbringing.

As Jocelyn grew older, her ambitions became more defined. She began to dream of a life far removed from the quiet, predictable existence of Lausanne. Stories of Paris, Milan, and New York City, cultural capitals filled

with art, fashion, and excitement, captivated her
imagination.

Her ambition was not limited to material success;
Jocelyn was driven by a desire to redefine herself and
create a persona that aligned with her dreams. She saw
herself as more than just a girl from a small Swiss town,
she envisioned a future where she could move
seamlessly among the world's elite, a life filled with
opulence and influence.

Despite her ambitions, Jocelyn faced the challenges of
growing up in a conservative, structured society.
Expectations for women during the mid-20th century
often revolved around domestic roles, and her dreams of
a glamorous, independent life stood in stark contrast to
these norms.

Jocelyn's ability to persevere through these challenges
was a testament to her resilience. She was determined to
carve her own path, even if it meant defying societal
expectations and taking risks. This determination would

later be a defining trait as she navigated the highs and lows of her public life.

During her teenage years, Jocelyn began to understand the power of self-presentation. She observed how appearance and charisma could influence others, and she started to cultivate her own image. Small changes in her hairstyle, makeup, and clothing were early experiments in the art of reinvention, an art she would master in her later years.

These formative years also taught her the importance of adaptability. Whether through adjusting her style or learning new social skills, Jocelyn demonstrated an ability to navigate different environments and connect with people from various backgrounds.

By the time she reached her late teens, Jocelyn's ambitions had crystallized into a desire to leave Lausanne and explore the wider world. She recognized that her hometown, while beautiful and nurturing, could not offer the opportunities she sought. Her determination to escape was not born out of dissatisfaction with her roots but out of a belief that she was destined for more.

Jocelyn Wildenstein's childhood influences and ambitions shaped the trajectory of her life in profound ways. The modesty of her upbringing, combined with her exposure to beauty and culture, created a deep-seated desire for transformation and success. Her fascination with glamour and her ability to dream beyond her circumstances became the driving forces behind her journey from Lausanne to the global stage.

These early experiences were not just the foundation of Jocelyn's ambitions; they were the first steps in a lifelong quest for self-definition and reinvention. Her story, while extraordinary in its twists and turns, remains rooted in the simple yet powerful dreams of a girl who dared to imagine a life beyond the ordinary.

CHAPTER TWO: DREAMS OF GLAMOUR

Jocelyn Wildenstein's life story is, at its heart, a tale of aspiration and transformation. Her "Dreams of Glamour" were born in the serene yet modest setting of Lausanne, Switzerland, where the opulence of the world beyond seemed distant but irresistibly alluring. From a young age, Jocelyn cultivated a vision of a life filled with luxury, beauty, and influence, dreams that would propel her toward fame and fortune, but at a cost few could imagine.

Growing up in the 1940s and 1950s, Jocelyn was deeply influenced by the cultural icons of her time. Actresses like Grace Kelly, Marilyn Monroe, and Brigitte Bardot were more than just movie stars; they were embodiments of an unattainable ideal, elegant, glamorous, and adored by millions. Jocelyn was captivated by their polished appearances, lavish lifestyles, and the mystique that surrounded them.

European royalty, with their opulent jewels, grand palaces, and carefully curated public images, also fueled her imagination. Stories of glamorous parties in Paris, Milan, and Monaco became the fodder for her daydreams. These icons represented a world far removed from her modest Swiss upbringing, but one she believed she could reach with determination and reinvention.

The mid-20th century was an era of transformation in media and culture, with magazines, films, and television bringing the allure of glamour into homes worldwide. For Jocelyn, these outlets served as a window into a life of sophistication and elegance. She spent hours poring over glossy magazines like Vogue and Harper's Bazaar, studying the fashion, beauty trends, and social events that defined high society.

Movies were another powerful influence. Films depicting luxurious mansions, glamorous parties, and the charmed lives of the wealthy offered Jocelyn a glimpse of a lifestyle she yearned to experience. This exposure not only fed her dreams but also gave her a blueprint for how she might craft her own identity.

Even as a young girl, Jocelyn displayed a keen interest in aesthetics and presentation. She was drawn to the artistry of fashion and makeup, seeing them as tools for self-expression and transformation. Her mother's wardrobe and beauty accessories became a playground for Jocelyn's early experiments with style.

These experiments were more than just child's play; they were the seeds of a lifelong fascination with the power of appearance. Jocelyn came to understand that beauty and presentation could open doors and command attention, a lesson that would influence her later decisions regarding cosmetic surgery and self-image.

Though Lausanne was a city of cultural richness and natural beauty, it was also a place of restraint and conservatism. For Jocelyn, it often felt stifling, a setting that could not contain her growing ambitions. She longed for the excitement and grandeur of cities like

Paris, Milan, and New York, places where fashion, art, and high society thrived.

Jocelyn's dreams of glamour were not just about wealth or luxury; they were about transformation. She envisioned herself as someone who could transcend her modest beginnings and become part of an elite world. This desire to redefine herself, to create a new identity in line with her aspirations, became a driving force in her life.

In mid-20th-century Switzerland, social mobility was often limited, and one's place in society was largely determined by birth. Jocelyn was acutely aware of the barriers that separated her from the world she admired. However, she saw these barriers not as insurmountable but as challenges to overcome.

She believed that with the right image, connections, and determination, she could bridge the gap between her modest upbringing and the glamorous lifestyle she envisioned. This belief in the power of self-reinvention would later define her approach to life.

By her late teens, Jocelyn's dreams of glamour had evolved into a clear vision. She began to plan her escape from Lausanne, seeking opportunities to immerse herself in the sophisticated world she admired. She was determined to learn the social graces, fashion sense, and confidence required to navigate elite circles.

Her move to Paris marked the first step toward realizing her dreams. In the city of lights, Jocelyn encountered a world that aligned with her aspirations, boutiques filled with haute couture, soirées attended by the crème de la crème, and a culture that celebrated beauty and elegance.

As Jocelyn pursued her dreams, she began to understand that glamour often came at a cost. The world she admired was one of perfection, where appearances were meticulously curated and expectations were high. To succeed in this world, Jocelyn felt she needed to meet its exacting standards, even if it meant altering herself to fit its ideals.

This realization laid the groundwork for Jocelyn's later decisions regarding cosmetic surgery and self-transformation. Her quest for glamour was not just about outward appearances; it was about creating a persona that could command respect and admiration in the circles she aspired to join.

Jocelyn Wildenstein's dreams of glamour were more than idle fantasies; they were the foundation of her extraordinary life. They drove her to leave her hometown, to reinvent herself, and to pursue a vision of perfection that would captivate the world.

While her journey was not without its challenges and controversies, Jocelyn's determination to live life on her own terms remains a testament to the power of ambition. Her dreams of glamour were not just about achieving wealth or fame; they were about creating a life that reflected her deepest aspirations and desires.

In chasing those dreams, Jocelyn Wildenstein became a symbol of transformation, a woman who dared to reimagine herself and redefine what it meant to live a glamorous life.

2.1 Moving Beyond Small-Town Life

Jocelyn Wildenstein's journey from the serene, conservative confines of Lausanne, Switzerland, to the cosmopolitan elite circles of Paris, New York, and beyond represents one of the most dramatic arcs in her life. For Jocelyn, moving beyond small-town life was not just a physical transition; it was a profound personal reinvention driven by her ambition to break free from societal constraints and embrace a life of glamour, luxury, and influence.

Lausanne in the mid-20th century was a picturesque city that epitomized the Swiss values of order, tradition, and modesty. While it was a cultural hub in its own right, offering access to art, music, and nature, it lacked the dynamism and opportunities of major global cities. For Jocelyn, the quiet predictability of Lausanne became a gilded cage, stifling her aspirations for something more.

Social norms in her community were deeply conservative, with clear expectations for women to follow traditional roles centered on family and domestic life. Jocelyn, however, was not content to conform to these expectations. From a young age, she displayed a restless curiosity and a yearning for a world where she could define herself on her own terms.

Jocelyn's decision to leave Lausanne was a pivotal moment in her life. While many people from her background might have found comfort in the stability and familiarity of small-town life, Jocelyn was determined to escape. Her desire to experience the excitement of the larger world outweighed any fears of the unknown.

Her early travels across Europe exposed her to new cultures, ideas, and lifestyles. Paris, in particular, became a symbol of freedom and possibility for Jocelyn. The city's vibrant fashion scene, intellectual discourse, and endless opportunities for reinvention resonated deeply with her ambitions.

In Paris, Jocelyn began to immerse herself in a lifestyle that was worlds apart from her upbringing in Lausanne. She worked in various roles, including modeling, which gave her access to a network of influential people and introduced her to the art of self-presentation. These experiences were transformative, teaching her how to navigate elite social circles and cultivate an image that aligned with her aspirations.

Paris also exposed Jocelyn to the power of reinvention. She observed how individuals in the city's fashion, art, and entertainment industries crafted their identities to achieve success. This understanding of self-reinvention would later become a cornerstone of Jocelyn's approach to life and her public persona.

Moving beyond small-town life also meant building relationships with people who could help Jocelyn achieve her dreams. In Paris and later in New York, Jocelyn developed a talent for networking. Her ability to adapt to different social environments and connect with influential individuals opened doors to opportunities that would have been unimaginable in Lausanne.

Through her connections, Jocelyn gained access to the world of high society, where she encountered wealthy entrepreneurs, artists, and other prominent figures. These relationships not only provided her with financial and social opportunities but also reinforced her belief in the power of ambition and self-presentation.

One of Jocelyn's greatest strengths during this period was her adaptability. Moving from a small town to major global cities required her to quickly learn new social norms, languages, and customs. Jocelyn's ability to blend into different environments and charm those around her became one of her defining traits.

She also learned how to leverage her unique background to her advantage. While she came from modest beginnings, Jocelyn used her Swiss upbringing as a foundation for her elegance and poise. Her refinement and cultural awareness made her stand out in elite circles, earning her respect and admiration.

While Jocelyn's move beyond small-town life was driven by ambition, it was also part of a deeper quest for identity. She was not just seeking material wealth or social status; she was searching for a way to define herself outside the limitations of her upbringing.

This quest for identity was reflected in her evolving appearance, social relationships, and personal ambitions. Jocelyn understood that moving beyond small-town life required more than physical relocation, it required a reinvention of who she was and what she represented.

Despite her successes, Jocelyn's transition to a cosmopolitan lifestyle was not without challenges.

Adapting to the fast-paced, competitive world of high society demanded resilience and determination. Jocelyn faced scrutiny, criticism, and the pressure to constantly maintain an image of perfection.

She also grappled with the emotional toll of leaving behind her roots. While she rarely spoke about her early life, it's clear that her upbringing in Lausanne remained a part of her, even as she embraced a new identity. This duality, being both the girl from a small Swiss town and the glamorous socialite, would shape her perspective on life and relationships.

By the time Jocelyn established herself in New York, she had fully transitioned from her small-town beginnings to a life of international prominence. Her marriage to billionaire Alec Wildenstein and her involvement in the art and fashion worlds solidified her place in elite society.

While the world often focused on her physical transformations and lavish lifestyle, Jocelyn's journey was fundamentally about the courage to dream beyond her circumstances and the determination to make those dreams a reality.

Jocelyn Wildenstein's story of moving beyond small-town life is a testament to the power of ambition, adaptability, and reinvention. Her decision to leave Lausanne was not just a geographical change but a symbolic break from a life of limitations.

Her journey serves as a reminder that the pursuit of one's dreams often requires stepping into the unknown and embracing the challenges of transformation. For Jocelyn, moving beyond small-town life was not just about escaping her past, it was about creating a future that aligned with her vision of who she wanted to be.

2.2 Early Relationships and Stepping into High Society

Jocelyn Wildenstein's ascent into high society was not simply a result of wealth or status, it was a carefully constructed journey that involved key relationships, calculated decisions, and an acute awareness of the social dynamics she was entering. As Jocelyn stepped into the glamorous, high-profile circles of New York and Paris, she navigated the complexities of social connections and personal reinvention with both precision and instinct. These early relationships, both romantic and professional, played a crucial role in shaping her transformation into the woman who would become an international figure known for her remarkable metamorphosis.

After leaving the small town of Lausanne and moving to Paris, Jocelyn found herself deeply immersed in the world of culture, fashion, and sophistication. In Paris, she observed the world she had always dreamed of, luxury, high fashion, powerful personalities, and an almost magical aura of exclusivity. She was both a participant in and an admirer of the haute couture and art scenes, but it wasn't long before she realized that the keys to entering high society required more than just admiration. They required strategic relationships and alliances with those already entrenched in these elite circles.

Jocelyn knew she needed more than beauty and ambition, she needed the right people to open doors for her, to provide her with the connections, opportunities, and social standing necessary for a future in high society. The first steps into this world would involve finding influential partners and individuals who could give her a legitimate place at the table.

One of the most pivotal relationships in Jocelyn's journey to high society was her marriage to Alec Wildenstein, an extraordinarily wealthy and powerful businessman who was heir to a vast fortune built from his family's art dealing empire. Alec was an influential figure with extensive social connections, and his wealth and status gave him access to some of the world's most exclusive circles.

Jocelyn met Alec in the early 1970s in Paris, and their relationship quickly evolved into a romance that captured the public's attention. Alec's family, known for their influence in the art world and the global elite, was the gateway to the society Jocelyn had long dreamed of entering. This relationship offered Jocelyn the opportunity to move from the fringes of high society to its center, where she could mingle with royals, political figures, celebrities, and other power brokers.

In marrying Alec Wildenstein in 1978, Jocelyn secured her place in one of the most elite social circles. The Wildenstein family, particularly Alec, was deeply involved in the international art scene, and their wealth was renowned in the worlds of business and cultural patronage. Through Alec, Jocelyn gained access to an entirely new social stratosphere, one that seemed worlds away from her humble beginnings in Lausanne.

The marriage, though personal, also had a profound social function for Jocelyn. It was her entry ticket into high society and the gilded world she had long admired. While their early life together was centered in Paris, Alec Wildenstein's vast wealth was primarily tied to his holdings in New York City, where the family operated one of the most prestigious art galleries in the world. After the marriage, Jocelyn made the significant move to New York, a city that represented the pinnacle of luxury and power in America.

In New York, Jocelyn immersed herself in the world of art, fashion, and philanthropy. It was a city where reputation and connections often trumped wealth, and Jocelyn understood that cultivating the right image and relationships was just as important as her husband's financial success.

She quickly became a fixture in New York's most glamorous social scenes. Whether at gallery openings, charity events, or high-profile parties, Jocelyn's new life centered around the glittering elite of the city. Her physical beauty and poised demeanor made her stand out, but it was her ability to network and forge connections that allowed her to thrive in these circles.

Jocelyn learned to align herself with the city's most influential figures. She forged friendships with powerful women, including socialites, artists, and philanthropists, who shared her passion for refinement and style. These women were not just friends but allies, offering advice and opportunities that would help Jocelyn move further into the heart of New York's elite social life.

Becoming part of high society meant Jocelyn had to learn the intricate social dynamics that governed these elite circles. Reputation, manners, and self-presentation were of utmost importance, and Jocelyn quickly learned that every gesture, conversation, and appearance counted. She honed her ability to blend into these circles with ease, adapting to the behaviors and expectations of the high society she had once only dreamed of.

She understood the power of exclusivity, knowing which events to attend, which people to be seen with, and how to create an aura of mystique around her own life. Jocelyn's keen sense of how to maintain an air of elegance and mystery allowed her to carve out a significant role for herself in New York's upper echelons.

At the same time, she was aware of the precarious nature of her position. Social hierarchies were rigid, and Jocelyn knew that she would need to constantly prove herself and align herself with the right figures to maintain her place. In this way, her relationships in New York became a vital element of her success, shaping not just her social reputation but also her personal identity.

For Jocelyn, relationships were never static; they were instruments for transformation. Early on, she realized that moving up in the world required more than just traditional networking, it required a continual reinvention of herself. Whether through her relationship with Alec Wildenstein or her friendships with other high society figures, Jocelyn's personal image evolved in a way that allowed her to embody the ideals of beauty, wealth, and sophistication.

Her marriage to Alec, in particular, allowed her to step into a new version of herself, one that embraced the lifestyle, values, and expectations of New York's high society. She reinvented her appearance, mannerisms, and even her social role, gradually shifting from a young woman with modest beginnings to a refined socialite and the epitome of glamour.

Her early relationships thus served as both stepping stones and transformative processes. They enabled Jocelyn to not only enter high society but to fundamentally alter her identity and position within it. These relationships empowered her to create a new narrative for herself, a narrative that revolved around wealth, beauty, and high status.

The dynamics of Jocelyn's early relationships also played a role in shaping the public and private personas she would eventually cultivate. While her relationship with Alec Wildenstein brought her into the public eye, her socialite friends and connections in the art world helped solidify her status as a figure of fascination.

As a result, Jocelyn learned the delicate balance between maintaining privacy and showcasing an image of wealth and sophistication. Her private life, particularly her relationship with Alec, became a symbol of her success, while her public appearances, whether at events or in the media, helped solidify her as a glamorous, high-society figure.

The relationships Jocelyn formed in these early years not only shaped her social standing but also influenced her personal life and decisions in the years to come. The art of creating and maintaining strategic relationships would remain central to Jocelyn's identity as she continued to navigate the complexities of high society. These relationships helped Jocelyn stay relevant in a world where appearances and connections often defined a person's worth, and they would become the cornerstone of the socialite and icon she would later become.

In stepping into high society, Jocelyn Wildenstein redefined herself and her destiny. The relationships she forged, both personal and professional, were integral to her transformation into a prominent figure in the world she had long admired. Through these connections, Jocelyn was able to move from the fringes of society to its glittering core, where her ambition, beauty, and social acumen propelled her to the heights of success.

CHAPTER THREE: MEETING ALEC WILDENSTEIN

Jocelyn Wildenstein's meeting with Alec Wildenstein, one of the wealthiest and most influential figures in the global art world, would prove to be one of the defining moments of her life. It was not simply a romantic encounter, but the catalyst for a monumental shift in her social standing, personal identity, and access to the elite circles she had long dreamed of joining.

Their meeting would not only set the course for a high-profile marriage but also introduce Jocelyn to a world that she had admired from afar and aspired to be a part of. This relationship would eventually become the central force that shaped her public persona and ignited her transformation into a media sensation.

By the time Jocelyn met Alec, she had already embarked on a journey of self-reinvention. Having grown up in the quiet, conservative town of Lausanne, Switzerland,

Jocelyn was aware of the social barriers that kept her from the glamorous, high-society world she longed to enter.

Her early life in Switzerland, while idyllic in many ways, was constricted by traditional gender roles and limited opportunities for women in her social class. Jocelyn's deep fascination with the allure of luxury, beauty, and high society had been nurtured since her youth, and by the time she reached Paris, she was ready to take bold steps to transform herself.

Jocelyn had already begun carving out a path that would lead her to the world of the rich and famous. She had worked in various roles, including as a model, and had immersed herself in the world of Parisian fashion and art.

But her social standing remained tethered to her modest origins, and she knew that entering the most exclusive circles of wealth and influence would require more than just hard work or aesthetic beauty, it would require the right connections. It was in this context that Jocelyn crossed paths with Alec Wildenstein, a man who embodied the epitome of the social and financial world she had dreamed of.

The Wildenstein family was a name that carried weight in both the business and art worlds. Alec's father, Daniel Wildenstein, had been a highly influential art dealer and the founder of one of the most prestigious art galleries in the world, dealing in some of the most sought-after artworks from the 19th and 20th centuries.

The Wildenstein family had long been associated with wealth, power, and art, establishing a legacy that spanned generations. Alec, the eldest son, had inherited not only his family's fortune but also its connections to some of the most prominent figures in global art, culture, and high society.

For Jocelyn, Alec was the embodiment of the very world she had been longing to enter. He was a well-established, charismatic figure who commanded attention wherever he went. With his family's wealth and social prominence, Alec had access to the world's most powerful circles, and his name alone could open doors that would otherwise remain closed. Alec's reputation as a leading art dealer and his position in New York's elite social scene made him an incredibly desirable figure for Jocelyn, he was both a gateway into the high society she dreamed of and a potential partner who could help her elevate her own status.

Jocelyn and Alec first met in Paris in the mid-1970s, at a time when both were navigating the complex social landscapes of the city. Paris, a hub of art, culture, and sophistication, was a natural meeting ground for individuals from all over the world who shared an appreciation for luxury, beauty, and refinement. Jocelyn, by this point, had already positioned herself within the fashionable circles of Paris and was beginning to gain recognition as a model and socialite. Alec, already established in his family's art business, frequented the city's high-end events and galleries.

The two met at an art exhibition, where Alec was captivated by Jocelyn's striking beauty and magnetic presence. Jocelyn, in turn, was drawn to Alec's refined manner and his deep knowledge of the art world. At the time, Alec was in his mid-40s, a seasoned socialite who had already experienced the power and privileges of wealth, while Jocelyn, in her late 20s, was a rising star, beautiful, ambitious, and eager to make her mark in the world.

Despite their age difference and differing backgrounds, there was an immediate attraction between the two. Alec was intrigued by Jocelyn's charm and elegance, while she was captivated by his wealth, power, and the promise of an entirely new life. What began as a chance encounter quickly blossomed into a whirlwind romance that would change the course of both of their lives.

For Jocelyn, Alec represented more than just a romantic partner. He symbolized the key to the high-society life she had long dreamed of, one that was characterized by opulence, influence, and social prominence. Alec's lifestyle was one that few could comprehend, and even fewer could access. His vast art collection, luxurious residences in Paris and New York, and ties to political and cultural elites placed him at the center of the world Jocelyn had been aspiring to join.

Alec was also known for his charm and charisma, traits that made him a prominent figure in New York and international social circles. His magnetic personality and his ability to navigate the highest levels of society were qualities that Jocelyn admired deeply. Beyond his wealth, it was his ability to blend in seamlessly with the world of the rich and famous that captivated her. For Jocelyn, Alec represented an opportunity to become part of that world, to step into the limelight, and to create a life she had once only fantasized about.

As their relationship developed, Alec became not just a romantic partner but a mentor of sorts for Jocelyn, introducing her to a world of influence and luxury she had never before experienced. Through Alec, Jocelyn gained access to the most exclusive circles, meeting world-renowned artists, aristocrats, politicians, and celebrities.

Their social life became one filled with grand galas, private art showings, and luxurious vacations to exotic locations. Alec's connections gave Jocelyn the opportunity to build relationships with powerful individuals, further cementing her place in the high society she had so long admired.

As their romance deepened, Alec and Jocelyn spent increasing amounts of time together, both in Paris and New York. Their relationship was not just based on love but also on mutual ambition. Alec's wealth and social standing opened up countless opportunities for Jocelyn, while her beauty, charm, and ambition helped elevate Alec's already glamorous public image.

In 1978, after several years of dating, Alec and Jocelyn Wildenstein married in a private ceremony, marking the beginning of a new chapter in both their lives. Their union was not just a personal one but a strategic alliance that would significantly elevate Jocelyn's social and financial status. As the wife of Alec Wildenstein, Jocelyn gained access to the rarefied world of the international elite, art collectors, business magnates, and socialites from across the globe.

While Jocelyn's beauty and charm had already captured Alec's heart, it was her willingness to embrace his world that ultimately made her indispensable to him. Together, they became a powerful duo in New York's social scene, known for their extravagant lifestyle, their shared passion for art, and their magnetic personalities.

However, it was not just the material gains from this marriage that defined their relationship; it was also the profound impact Alec had on Jocelyn's own sense of identity. Through him, she not only entered the world of high society but also began the process of transforming herself into a figure of glamour and sophistication. Alec, in many ways, became her mentor and enabler, helping her craft the image that would make her a household name.

Meeting Alec Wildenstein was more than just a serendipitous moment in Jocelyn's life, it was the beginning of her journey into the highest echelons of society, a world that she had dreamed of but had never truly believed she could access. Through Alec, Jocelyn not only entered a world of wealth and power but also began the process of reinventing herself, crafting a new identity that aligned with her ambition and aspirations.

The relationship with Alec Wildenstein set the stage for the next phase of Jocelyn's life, one that would involve fame, fortune, and a transformation that would captivate the public's imagination. As she entered this new world, she was no longer the young woman from Lausanne, Switzerland; she was the glamorous wife of one of the wealthiest men in the world, a figure poised to make her mark on both high society and the media.

3.1 The Whirlwind Romance

The romance between Jocelyn Wildenstein and Alec Wildenstein was one that seemed destined for the headlines, filled with passion, grandeur, and a sense of urgency. It was not merely a love story but the union of two worlds: one of ambition, beauty, and new beginnings, and the other of wealth, power, and established legacy.

Their whirlwind romance not only marked the beginning of a new chapter for both individuals but also set the stage for Jocelyn's eventual transformation into a media icon. It was a romance that transcended the ordinary, enveloped in the kind of exclusivity and glamour that would later define Jocelyn's public persona.

Jocelyn and Alec's paths first crossed in Paris during the 1970s, a time when the city was a magnet for artists, socialites, and wealthy heirs. Paris, as the epicenter of culture, art, and fashion, was the perfect backdrop for a romance that would go on to captivate the world. For

Jocelyn, the city represented both the fulfillment of her dreams and a launchpad for her aspirations. Alec, by contrast, was already firmly entrenched in the world of luxury, with his family's art empire allowing him to move among the most powerful figures in Europe and America.

At the time they met, Jocelyn was a rising star in the Parisian social scene, already beginning to establish herself as a model and socialite. Alec, though nearly two decades older than her, was equally prominent in his own circles, known not just for his wealth, but also for his charismatic presence at the most exclusive events. The chemistry between them was instant, and their attraction to each other was undeniable.

Alec was captivated by Jocelyn's beauty, her poise, and her effortless charm. He was a man who had already lived through many phases of wealth and privilege, but Jocelyn was different from the women he had encountered before. She was ambitious, eager, and yet untouched by the pressures of the high-society world he knew so well. For Jocelyn, Alec embodied everything she had ever dreamed of a powerful man with access to the highest levels of wealth and influence. He was the gateway to the world she longed to be a part of, a world where art, culture, and prestige were paramount.

The early stages of their relationship were marked by a magnetic pull between the two, driven by their differences as much as their similarities. While Alec was already well-established in his career and status, Jocelyn was still building her identity, seeking to position herself in the highest echelons of society. This created a dynamic of mentor and mentee, but also one of mutual admiration. Alec was drawn to Jocelyn's ambition and her youthful energy, while Jocelyn found Alec's sophistication and knowledge of the elite world both inspiring and intoxicating.

Their whirlwind romance was punctuated by lavish nights out, intimate dinners, and private gatherings at art galleries, where Alec's vast collection of paintings and sculptures was on display. These moments were not only filled with romance but also with the promise of a new life for Jocelyn, one in which she could embrace her desires for wealth and prestige without reservation.

Alec's influence allowed Jocelyn to step deeper into the world of New York's social elite, where she was introduced to a host of influential people, including celebrities, art collectors, politicians, and other socialites. The places they frequented were luxurious, private parties in grand mansions, art auctions at Christie's, and intimate gatherings with the rich and famous. Alec had the keys to this world, and he was eager to share it with Jocelyn, who seemed like a perfect fit for this new realm of wealth and social prestige.

What made their romance especially whirlwind-like was the speed with which it progressed. Within just a few months of meeting, Jocelyn and Alec's relationship became intensely serious. Their whirlwind romance was not marked by a slow courtship or long stretches of dating, but rather by an immediate connection that quickly became all-consuming.

Jocelyn, who had long dreamed of being a part of the elite social circles, was swept off her feet by Alec's charm, wealth, and the doors he could open for her. For Alec, Jocelyn's beauty and vivacity were irresistible, and her ability to adapt to the high-society world he knew so well made her the ideal companion. The connection between them felt both exciting and fated. Their union was one of mutual benefit, a romance that intertwined both love and opportunity.

The rapid progression of their relationship shocked many who knew them, especially given the substantial age gap between the two. Alec was 46, while Jocelyn was just 28 at the time they began dating. The difference in their ages only served to fuel public curiosity and speculation, adding a layer of intrigue to their already glamorous relationship. Despite the age difference, their romance was a striking example of how, for both parties, the bond transcended physical appearance and wealth, instead focusing on shared ambition and common goals.

Jocelyn's romance with Alec was transformative, marking the beginning of a dramatic shift in her life. While she had long dreamed of joining the elite circles of society, it was through her relationship with Alec that she began to truly see the doorways open before her. Alec's connections introduced her to the best of what the world had to offer, luxury, influence, and fame. But it wasn't just about entering a new world; it was about transforming into a version of herself that could not only participate in this world but also thrive within it.

As their relationship grew more serious, Jocelyn began to reinvent herself in ways that would be both subtle and dramatic. She became more attuned to the expectations of high society, refining her mannerisms, her fashion sense, and her public image. The world that Alec inhabited required a certain type of woman, elegant, poised, and sophisticated, and Jocelyn embraced this role with great determination.

The more time she spent with Alec, the more she adapted to his world. Her appearance shifted, her lifestyle evolved, and she was no longer the young woman from Lausanne but an emerging socialite who was stepping into her new role as a wife in one of the wealthiest families in the world.

Alec, for his part, was supportive of Jocelyn's transformation. He encouraged her to develop her own sense of style and to become a more polished version of herself. Together, they became a power couple, one whose name was soon whispered in the most exclusive circles of New York, Paris, and beyond.

The speed and intensity of their relationship culminated in a whirlwind engagement. After just two years of dating, Alec proposed to Jocelyn in the early months of 1978. The proposal itself was as grand as the romance that preceded it. Alec, ever the art lover, proposed with a diamond ring that was fit for a woman destined to live a life of luxury. The ring was not just a symbol of their love but also of the life of excess and glamour that they would share together.

Their wedding was nothing short of spectacular, a private, extravagant ceremony that was held in one of the Wildenstein family's opulent estates. The guest list was a who's who of New York's elite, including artists, businessmen, celebrities, and political figures. Jocelyn, now the wife of one of the wealthiest men in the world, was dressed in a couture gown that highlighted her transformation into a sophisticated, glamorous woman.

Their marriage, which made headlines around the world, solidified their status as one of the most prominent power couples in the international elite. Jocelyn's transformation into a glamorous socialite was complete. No longer the aspiring model from Lausanne, she had now become a force in her own right, with Alec by her side to navigate the complexities of high society.

Jocelyn and Alec's whirlwind romance left an indelible mark not only on their lives but also on the media and public perception. Their relationship became a symbol of both the power of love and the allure of wealth. For Jocelyn, it was the beginning of a new identity, one that was tightly intertwined with Alec's wealth, status, and social connections. For Alec, it was a partnership that offered not just companionship but also a means to continue his family's legacy in the spotlight.

Though their marriage would eventually face tumultuous challenges and end in a highly publicized divorce, the early years of their romance laid the foundation for Jocelyn's transformation into one of the most talked-about women of the 20th century. The whirlwind romance was not just a love story, it was the moment that set the stage for a life of glamour, media scrutiny, and a legacy that would be remembered for its extraordinary highs and eventual dramatic lows.

3.2 Marriage into a Legacy of Wealth and Art

When Jocelyn Wildenstein married Alec Wildenstein in 1978, she stepped into a world of extraordinary privilege, power, and cultural significance. The Wildenstein family name was synonymous with wealth and art, possessing one of the most prestigious private art collections in the world and operating a centuries-old business that wielded influence across continents. For Jocelyn, this union was not just a marriage; it was an induction into a legacy that would redefine her life and anchor her firmly within the global elite.

The Wildenstein family's wealth and status were rooted in their unparalleled dominance of the art world. The family dynasty began in the late 19th century with Nathan Wildenstein, a French art dealer who founded the Wildenstein Institute, an art dealership and research organization that would become the gold standard in its field. Over generations, the family built an empire that specialized in Old Masters, Impressionist, and Post-Impressionist works, creating an exclusive network of collectors, museums, and institutions.

By the time Jocelyn married Alec, the Wildenstein family was a cornerstone of the international art scene. Their collection, valued in the billions, included iconic works by artists like Rembrandt, Van Gogh, Monet, and

Cézanne. In addition to art, the family owned sprawling properties, including mansions in New York and Paris, a luxurious apartment in Monte Carlo, and a 66,000-acre Kenyan wildlife reserve.

Jocelyn's marriage to Alec was a turning point that ushered her into a life of unimaginable luxury. As Alec's wife, she became part of a family that lived at the intersection of art, business, and high society. The expectations placed upon her were immense, as she was now a public face of a dynasty that prided itself on its exclusivity and sophistication.

The Wildensteins were known for their discretion and their ability to navigate the art world with a combination of elegance and shrewdness. Jocelyn quickly adapted to this environment, learning to balance the dual roles of being Alec's partner and a representative of the family's legacy. Her responsibilities extended beyond being a wife; she was expected to embody the values and image of the Wildenstein name.

Jocelyn's marriage afforded her access to a level of wealth that few could comprehend. Her lifestyle was one of constant opulence, characterized by private jets, couture wardrobes, and residences adorned with priceless artworks. The Wildenstein properties, each a masterpiece of architecture and design, were showcases of the family's taste and affluence.

One of the most notable estates was the Ol Jogi Wildlife Conservancy in Kenya, a property that combined luxury with conservation. The sprawling estate featured a mansion with a private zoo, helicopter pads, and breathtaking views of the African savannah. Jocelyn, who had always been drawn to exotic locations and wildlife, found a sense of fulfillment in this environment. She embraced the role of hostess, entertaining guests from around the world with grand safaris and lavish gatherings.

Art was at the center of the Wildenstein family's identity, and Jocelyn's marriage to Alec immersed her in this world. Alec, deeply entrenched in the art business, frequently involved Jocelyn in the family's dealings, whether it was attending high-profile auctions, meeting with collectors, or hosting exhibitions. Jocelyn quickly developed a refined appreciation for art, gaining insight into its history, provenance, and market value.

The Wildensteins' collection was not merely decorative; it was a strategic asset that reinforced their power and influence. Jocelyn learned that the art world was as much about prestige and connections as it was about beauty and creativity. Being part of this legacy required her to navigate complex social and professional networks, cementing her position within a rarefied circle of collectors, curators, and art historians.

While Jocelyn's marriage brought her immense wealth and status, it also came with significant challenges. The Wildensteins were a family steeped in tradition, with rigid expectations about how their name and legacy should be preserved. Jocelyn's marriage to Alec placed her under intense scrutiny, both within the family and in the broader social sphere.

The Wildensteins were known for their insular nature, valuing privacy and loyalty above all else. Jocelyn, who was naturally outgoing and ambitious, sometimes struggled to align with these values. Her vibrant personality and desire for public recognition occasionally clashed with the family's preference for discretion. This tension would later play a role in the unraveling of her marriage and her subsequent legal battles with the family.

Despite the challenges, Jocelyn embraced the opportunities that her marriage provided. She used her newfound status to redefine herself, transforming from an ambitious young woman from Lausanne into a sophisticated socialite and global icon. With Alec by her side, she became a fixture in the upper echelons of society, attending galas, charity events, and art openings.

Jocelyn's transformation was not just external; it was also deeply personal. She saw herself as an active participant in the Wildenstein legacy, contributing to its ongoing story through her public presence and support of Alec's ventures. Her marriage was a partnership, one that combined love with a shared commitment to maintaining and expanding the family's influence.

Jocelyn's marriage to Alec was more than a union of two individuals; it was a fusion of ambition, tradition, and wealth. Together, they represented the ideal of a power couple, their lives intertwined with the art and culture that defined the Wildenstein name. For Jocelyn, marrying into this legacy was both a dream realized and a challenge undertaken, a step that would forever shape her identity and her place in the world.

Though the marriage would eventually be marred by controversy and legal battles, its early years were a testament to the transformative power of love, ambition, and the allure of an extraordinary legacy. Jocelyn's journey into the Wildenstein family remains one of the most compelling chapters in her story, offering a glimpse into a world where art and wealth converge to create a life of unparalleled opulence and complexity.

CHAPTER FOUR: LIFE AT THE PARK

The years following Jocelyn Wildenstein's marriage to Alec Wildenstein were a time of unparalleled luxury, influence, and prominence. With access to immense wealth, a legendary art collection, and a global network of elites, Jocelyn found herself at the pinnacle of high society. These years, defined by glamour, opulence, and privilege, represented the apex of her life. It was a time when she fully embraced her role as Alec's wife and a figure in her own right, leaving an indelible mark on the social and cultural fabric of the era.

Life at the peak for Jocelyn was defined by a lifestyle of almost unimaginable luxury. The Wildenstein wealth afforded her every conceivable indulgence, from private jets and couture fashion to lavish estates across multiple continents. Jocelyn and Alec were fixtures in exclusive social circles, regularly attending galas, art auctions, and high-society events in cities like New York, Paris, and Monte Carlo.

One of the most iconic aspects of Jocelyn's life at this time was her wardrobe. She became known for her bold fashion choices, favoring designers like Yves Saint Laurent, Chanel, and Dior. Her style was a blend of classic elegance and dramatic flair, reflecting her personality and her aspirations. Jocelyn's fashion was not just about beauty; it was a statement of her position in the world.

Beyond fashion, Jocelyn's days were filled with luxurious routines. She frequented the finest spas, dined at Michelin-starred restaurants, and vacationed at exclusive resorts. Her lifestyle was a seamless blend of leisure and spectacle, where every moment was an opportunity to showcase her privileged existence.

One of the hallmarks of Jocelyn's life at the peak was her access to the Wildenstein family's sprawling properties. Each estate was a masterpiece of design and opulence, serving as both a private retreat and a symbol of the family's wealth.

The family's New York townhouse was a centerpiece of their social life. Located in Manhattan's Upper East Side, the townhouse was an architectural marvel, adorned with priceless artworks and antiques. Here, Jocelyn and Alec hosted glittering parties attended by celebrities, politicians, and art collectors.

Another significant property was the Ol Jogi Wildlife Conservancy in Kenya, a 66,000-acre estate that blended luxury with nature. This African sanctuary was one of Jocelyn's favorite places, offering a unique combination of breathtaking landscapes, exotic wildlife, and extravagant accommodations. Jocelyn took pride in hosting guests at Ol Jogi, treating them to private safaris, sumptuous feasts, and a glimpse into the Wildenstein family's unparalleled lifestyle.

As part of the Wildenstein family, Jocelyn was deeply immersed in the world of art. The family's collection, valued in the billions, included works by some of the greatest artists in history. Jocelyn attended auctions at Christie's and Sotheby's, mingling with collectors and

The price of perfection

curators while expanding her knowledge of art history and market trends.

Art was not just a passion but also a strategic tool for the Wildensteins. Their collection bolstered their status as tastemakers and cultural arbiters. Jocelyn understood the power of art in shaping public perception and worked alongside Alec to maintain the family's influence in this exclusive sphere.

Jocelyn's involvement in the art world also extended to philanthropy. She supported cultural initiatives, donated to museums, and participated in charity events that blended art with social causes. These efforts further cemented her position as a respected figure in both the art world and high society.

Jocelyn's life at the peak was as much about socializing as it was about wealth and art. She thrived in the world of galas, charity balls, and high-profile events, where she mingled with the global elite. Jocelyn had a natural charisma that drew people to her, making her a sought-after guest and hostess.

Her social calendar was filled with events that reflected her status. From the Met Gala in New York to exclusive yacht parties in the Mediterranean, Jocelyn was a constant presence in the most glamorous settings. Her ability to navigate these environments with grace and confidence made her a prominent figure in the international social scene.

While Jocelyn's life at the peak was marked by unparalleled luxury, it also came with its challenges. The pressure to maintain her appearance and public image led her to undergo multiple cosmetic procedures, a choice that would later become a defining aspect of her story. Jocelyn's pursuit of physical perfection was driven by both personal desires and societal expectations, reflecting the complexities of her identity and the world she inhabited.

During these years, Jocelyn's identity expanded beyond being Alec's wife. She became a figure of intrigue and admiration, known for her beauty, style, and bold personality. Jocelyn was not content to simply exist in Alec's shadow; she carved out her own space in the world of high society, establishing herself as a woman of influence and distinction.

Her life at the peak was a testament to her determination and ability to adapt. Jocelyn had transformed from a young woman in Lausanne with dreams of glamour into a global icon who lived a life few could imagine.

Jocelyn Wildenstein's life at the peak represented the realization of her dreams and the culmination of her journey into the upper echelons of society. These years were marked by excess, beauty, and the allure of a life lived without limits.

However, the heights of her success also foreshadowed the challenges that lay ahead. As much as Jocelyn enjoyed her life at the peak, it was a world that demanded perfection and came with immense pressure. Despite the trials she would later face, these years remain a defining chapter in her extraordinary story—a time when she lived as a queen in a world of art, wealth, and glamour.

4.1 Lavish Living in Manhattan and Beyond

Jocelyn Wildenstein's life in Manhattan and her travels across the globe epitomized the pinnacle of luxury. The Wildenstein family's vast fortune and art empire afforded Jocelyn access to an opulent lifestyle few could imagine, spanning extravagant real estate, haute couture fashion, fine dining, and exclusive social events. Her lavish living, centered around Manhattan but extending to the far corners of the world, showcased her transformation into a global socialite and a figure synonymous with excess and glamour.

At the heart of Jocelyn's life was the Wildenstein family's stately townhouse in Manhattan's Upper East

Side. This iconic property was not just a home but a symbol of their immense wealth and social standing. Located in one of the most prestigious neighborhoods in New York City, the townhouse stood as a testament to the family's prominence in both the art world and high society.

Inside, the townhouse was a work of art in itself. The interiors were adorned with rare antiques, luxurious fabrics, and priceless artworks from the Wildenstein collection, including masterpieces by Rembrandt and Monet. Every room reflected a meticulous attention to detail, blending historical elegance with modern comfort. Crystal chandeliers illuminated grand halls, while custom-designed furniture added an air of exclusivity.

The townhouse also served as a venue for the Wildensteins' glamorous soirées. Jocelyn and Alec frequently hosted dinners, galas, and private art exhibitions, attracting an elite guest list that included celebrities, politicians, and global art collectors. These gatherings reinforced the family's reputation as cultural arbiters and tastemakers, with Jocelyn at the forefront as a gracious and captivating hostess.

While Manhattan served as her base, Jocelyn's life extended far beyond its borders. The Wildensteins' wealth allowed her to traverse the globe, enjoying the finest destinations and experiences that money could buy. Jocelyn traveled extensively, frequenting iconic luxury hubs such as Monte Carlo, Paris, London, and the French Riviera.

In Paris, the Wildenstein family's historic estate became another focal point of Jocelyn's life. This property, steeped in European charm, offered an intimate glimpse into the family's heritage. Jocelyn often spent time in the city attending fashion shows, art exhibitions, and charity events. Her presence at Parisian high society gatherings further cemented her image as a cosmopolitan icon.

Monte Carlo, with its dazzling casinos, yachts, and Mediterranean allure, was another favorite destination. Jocelyn embraced the glamorous lifestyle of this principality, mingling with royalty, business magnates, and fellow socialites. She was a regular fixture at the annual Monaco Grand Prix and other exclusive events, epitomizing the jet-setting lifestyle that defined her world.

One of the most unique aspects of Jocelyn's lavish life was her connection to the Ol Jogi Wildlife Conservancy in Kenya. This sprawling 66,000-acre property was more than just a luxurious retreat; it was a sanctuary that combined conservation with unparalleled opulence.

The estate featured a grand mansion equipped with every conceivable luxury, including a private zoo, helicopter pads, and infinity pools overlooking the savannah. Jocelyn was deeply involved in the estate's activities, hosting guests for private safaris and showcasing the property's rare and exotic wildlife.

Ol Jogi was a place where Jocelyn could blend her love for nature with her penchant for luxury. It was a rare escape from the bustling cities where she spent much of her time, offering her a sense of serenity while still reflecting the grandeur of her lifestyle.

Jocelyn's wardrobe was another hallmark of her lavish living. She was known for her bold and extravagant fashion choices, often wearing bespoke pieces from the world's most renowned designers. From Yves Saint Laurent and Chanel to Versace and Valentino, Jocelyn's closet was a treasure trove of haute couture.

Her fashion extended beyond clothing to include a dazzling collection of jewelry, featuring diamonds, emeralds, and rubies of extraordinary size and quality. Jocelyn's accessories were often custom-designed, reflecting her unique sense of style and her status as a global icon of luxury.

Every appearance Jocelyn made, whether at a Manhattan gala or an exclusive event in Europe, was a carefully curated spectacle. Her ability to blend elegance with audacity set her apart in the world of high fashion and solidified her place as a style icon of her time.

Jocelyn's social life revolved around the finest dining establishments and entertainment venues. In Manhattan, she frequented legendary restaurants such as Le Cirque and The Four Seasons, where she dined on gourmet cuisine crafted by world-class chefs.

Beyond dining, Jocelyn's evenings were often spent attending Broadway premieres, opera performances at the Metropolitan Opera House, and exclusive gallery openings. Her presence at these events was both a reflection of her personal interests and a statement of her cultural sophistication.

Jocelyn's global travels introduced her to a wide array of culinary delights and entertainment experiences. Whether it was dining at Michelin-starred restaurants in Paris or attending private concerts on the French Riviera, every experience was a celebration of the finer things in life.

Jocelyn's lifestyle placed her among the most elite circles in the world. Her friends and acquaintances included aristocrats, celebrities, business tycoons, and influential figures from the art world. Jocelyn's charm, charisma, and natural ability to navigate these circles made her a beloved figure in high society.

Her connections extended beyond social gatherings, as she often collaborated with influential individuals on philanthropic and cultural initiatives. These relationships reinforced her status as not just a participant in, but also a contributor to, the global elite lifestyle.

While Jocelyn's lavish living brought her immense joy and fulfillment, it also came with challenges. Maintaining such a lifestyle required constant effort and significant resources, placing pressure on her personal and professional relationships. The expectations of high society often demanded perfection, leaving little room for vulnerability or missteps.

Jocelyn's pursuit of beauty and glamour also led her to undergo numerous cosmetic procedures, which became a defining and controversial aspect of her public image. This quest for physical perfection reflected both the privileges and the pressures of her extraordinary life.

Jocelyn Wildenstein's life in Manhattan and beyond remains a vivid example of what it means to live at the height of wealth and privilege. Her experiences, from the splendor of her Manhattan townhouse to the exotic allure of Ol Jogi, encapsulate a world of excess and aspiration.

Though her story would later take a more tumultuous turn, the years she spent embracing lavish living were a testament to her determination, ambition, and ability to thrive in a world few could navigate. For Jocelyn, this chapter of her life was not just about material wealth, it was about creating a legacy of elegance, influence, and unforgettable experiences.

4.2 Horses, Yachts, and Private Jets

Jocelyn Wildenstein's life was a dazzling tableau of wealth and extravagance, and few symbols embodied this more than her deep involvement with horses, yachts, and private jets. These luxuries not only reflected her extraordinary lifestyle but also showcased her passions, ambitions, and her position in the upper echelons of society. From her equestrian pursuits to glamorous voyages across oceans and skies, Jocelyn's connection to these lavish symbols of affluence was as personal as it was public.

Horses held a special place in Jocelyn's life, long before her ascent to international fame. Growing up in Lausanne, Switzerland, she developed a love for riding, a passion that blossomed into a lifelong affair with equestrian culture.

Upon marrying Alec Wildenstein, Jocelyn's relationship with horses took on a new dimension. The Wildenstein family owned and bred some of the most prestigious racehorses in the world, and their involvement in the equestrian industry was both a business and a way of life. Jocelyn quickly embraced this world, immersing herself in the intricacies of horse breeding, training, and racing.

The Wildensteins' thoroughbred breeding operation was legendary, producing numerous champions that competed in elite races across Europe and the United States. Jocelyn became a familiar face at events like the Prix de l'Arc de Triomphe in Paris and the Kentucky Derby in the United States, where she mingled with aristocrats, celebrities, and fellow horse enthusiasts.

Jocelyn's connection to horses extended beyond the racetrack. She was known for her elegant equestrian attire and her ability to ride with grace and confidence. Her passion for horses was not merely about status; it was a genuine love that tied her to a centuries-old tradition of equestrian excellence.

Yachts were another hallmark of Jocelyn's luxurious lifestyle. The Wildensteins owned some of the most exquisite vessels, which they used for leisure, entertainment, and international travel. For Jocelyn, yachting was not just a pastime; it was a way to experience the world in unparalleled comfort and style.

The yachts in Jocelyn's life were floating palaces, equipped with every conceivable amenity. These vessels featured opulent interiors, complete with marble floors, crystal chandeliers, and state-of-the-art entertainment systems. Spacious decks offered breathtaking views of the sea, while private chefs prepared gourmet meals tailored to the tastes of their guests.

Jocelyn spent countless summers cruising the Mediterranean, exploring destinations like Saint-Tropez, the Amalfi Coast, and the Greek islands. Her yacht trips were often accompanied by glamorous parties, where she entertained a mix of celebrities, business magnates, and members of high society. These gatherings, set against the backdrop of azure waters and golden sunsets, became legendary in their own right.

Yachting also allowed Jocelyn to escape the public eye and enjoy moments of privacy. Whether sunbathing on deck or swimming in secluded coves, she found solace in the tranquility of the open sea, a stark contrast to the fast-paced life she led on land.

Private jets were an essential part of Jocelyn's lifestyle, enabling her to traverse the globe with speed, comfort, and exclusivity. For someone constantly moving between New York, Paris, Monte Carlo, and Kenya, private aviation was not just a luxury, it was a necessity.

The jets Jocelyn used were equipped with lavish interiors that mirrored the opulence of her homes and yachts. Plush leather seats, custom-designed interiors, and gourmet catering ensured that every flight was an extension of her luxurious lifestyle. These jets were not merely a mode of transportation; they were a mobile sanctuary that allowed Jocelyn to maintain her standards of living even at 30,000 feet.

Private aviation also gave Jocelyn the freedom to travel on her terms. She could jet off to a secluded island on a whim or attend an important event in another country without the constraints of commercial air travel. This flexibility allowed her to seamlessly balance her social, professional, and personal commitments.

Jocelyn's use of private jets also played a role in her public image. Arriving at events via private jet was a statement of her wealth and influence, reinforcing her status as one of the world's most glamorous women.

For Jocelyn, horses, yachts, and private jets were more than symbols of affluence; they were extensions of her personality and passions. Her love for horses reflected her connection to nature and tradition, while her affinity for yachts and jets showcased her adventurous spirit and desire for freedom.

These luxuries also highlighted Jocelyn's ability to navigate the complex world of the global elite. Whether attending an equestrian event, hosting a yacht party, or jetting off to an exotic destination, she exuded confidence and sophistication, embodying the ideals of a high-society lifestyle.

While Jocelyn's life with horses, yachts, and private jets was enviable, it also came with its challenges. Maintaining such a lifestyle required immense resources, and the pressures of sustaining this level of luxury often strained her relationships and finances.

Moreover, these symbols of wealth occasionally attracted criticism, with some viewing them as excessive or disconnected from the realities faced by ordinary people. Jocelyn, however, remained unapologetic about her choices, embracing the life she had built and the opportunities it afforded her.

Jocelyn Wildenstein's association with horses, yachts, and private jets remains a defining aspect of her story.

These elements of her life reflect not only her extraordinary wealth but also her pursuit of a life filled with beauty, adventure, and passion.

From the racetracks of Paris to the Mediterranean's azure waters and the skies above Manhattan, Jocelyn lived a life that was as expansive as it was opulent. Her experiences with these symbols of luxury offer a glimpse into a world where dreams of grandeur are realized, leaving behind a legacy of extravagance that continues to fascinate and inspire.

CHAPTER FIVE: AN EYE FOR ART AND EXOTIC BEAUTY

Jocelyn Wildenstein's life was deeply intertwined with art and aesthetics, a connection that extended far beyond her status as a Wildenstein by marriage. Known for her striking persona and her often controversial cosmetic transformations, Jocelyn cultivated a distinctive appreciation for beauty, blending classic and exotic influences.

Her "eye for art" was not only influenced by her access to one of the world's most significant art collections but also by her personal fascination with rare and unconventional forms of beauty, which she pursued in both her lifestyle and physical appearance.

Marriage into the Wildenstein family, one of the most prominent names in the global art scene, offered Jocelyn unparalleled access to the art world. The Wildensteins owned one of the largest private art collections in the world, valued in the billions, encompassing works by masters like Monet, Rembrandt, and Cézanne. This immense wealth of art not only reflected the family's cultural sophistication but also positioned them as key players in art auctions, galleries, and museums.

Jocelyn's life in this world was one of constant exposure to beauty and creativity. She attended exclusive art auctions at Sotheby's and Christie's, mingled with collectors and curators, and participated in high-profile exhibitions. Her presence at these events was not just as Alec Wildenstein's wife; Jocelyn established herself as someone who deeply appreciated the nuances of art, often engaging with experts to understand the history and techniques behind the masterpieces she encountered.

Her time in this sphere broadened her artistic sensibilities and refined her taste. Jocelyn was particularly drawn to pieces that captured emotion, exotic landscapes, and unique perspectives. Her artistic preferences often mirrored her own life, vivid, bold, and unapologetically unique.

Jocelyn's fascination with beauty extended far beyond the art world into her own physical appearance. She became synonymous with dramatic cosmetic transformations, which she pursued over decades. Her surgeries were often described as an effort to achieve feline-like features, inspired by her love for big cats such as tigers and lions. This pursuit of exotic beauty was as much a personal journey as it was a public spectacle.

Her transformation was polarizing. Some viewed it as a bold expression of individuality, while others saw it as a cautionary tale about the extremes of cosmetic surgery. Jocelyn, however, was unapologetic about her choices. She saw her appearance as a canvas, much like the art she admired, and she wielded her transformations as a form of self-expression.

This fascination with the exotic also extended to her lifestyle. Jocelyn surrounded herself with rare and beautiful things, from African wildlife to intricate jewelry inspired by far-flung cultures. Her home décor often incorporated elements that reflected her love for nature and unique aesthetics, blending traditional opulence with an exotic flair.

Jocelyn's artistic sensibilities were evident in how she curated her living spaces. Her residences, including the iconic Manhattan townhouse and the Ol Jogi Wildlife Conservancy in Kenya, were filled with meticulously chosen décor that reflected her tastes. These spaces were adorned with everything from classical European antiques to artifacts from African and Asian cultures, creating a harmonious blend of global influences.

Her fashion choices also reflected her artistic vision. Jocelyn's wardrobe was a masterpiece in itself, featuring bespoke pieces from designers like Versace, Yves Saint Laurent, and Valentino. She often chose bold patterns, exotic fabrics, and dramatic silhouettes, making her a standout figure in the world of haute couture. Her jewelry, often custom-designed, incorporated elements like animal motifs and vibrant gemstones, further emphasizing her love for exotic beauty.

One of Jocelyn's most distinctive contributions to the art of living was her passion for wildlife and conservation, particularly at the Ol Jogi Wildlife Conservancy in Kenya. For Jocelyn, the natural world was a form of living art, filled with colors, patterns, and movements that rivaled any man-made masterpiece.

The conservancy itself was a blend of luxury and nature, featuring opulent interiors that complemented the breathtaking landscapes of the African savannah. Jocelyn's love for big cats and exotic animals was evident in the way she engaged with the wildlife, often treating them with the same reverence she had for priceless works of art. Her dedication to preserving these creatures reflected her belief that beauty, whether in art or nature, deserved to be cherished and protected.

Jocelyn's eye for art and beauty was inseparable from her identity. Whether through her involvement in the Wildenstein art empire, her dramatic physical transformations, or her appreciation for exotic and rare aesthetics, Jocelyn consistently sought to push boundaries and redefine norms.

Her journey was not without controversy, but it was undeniably one of courage and creativity. Jocelyn's choices, while polarizing, were a reflection of her belief that beauty is subjective and that it often requires daring to achieve something extraordinary.

Jocelyn Wildenstein's story is one of a woman who lived artfully, embracing the world's most extraordinary beauty while also crafting her own. Her life in the art world, combined with her unique aesthetic sensibilities, left a lasting impact on how beauty is perceived and pursued.

Though her dramatic transformations often overshadowed other aspects of her life, Jocelyn's eye for art and exotic beauty remains a testament to her individuality and vision. She lived boldly, unapologetically redefining what it means to be both a patron of art and a work of art herself.

5.1 Alec's Love for Big Cats

Alec Wildenstein, heir to one of the world's most
influential art dynasties, was a man of varied interests,
but few passions equaled his deep admiration for big
cats. This fascination went beyond mere appreciation; it
became a defining aspect of his identity and an integral
part of his relationship with Jocelyn Wildenstein. Alec's
love for big cats was woven into his lifestyle,
conservation efforts, and even his family dynamics,
shaping a unique legacy that extended far beyond his
immense wealth and prominence in the art world.

Alec's interest in big cats likely began in his youth,
nurtured by a life of privilege and access to exotic
experiences. Growing up in a family that owned
sprawling estates and mingled with the global elite, Alec
was exposed to rare and majestic animals from an early
age. His fascination with wildlife, particularly predators
like lions, tigers, and leopards, seemed to stem from their

strength, elegance, and untamed nature, qualities that mirrored his own ambitious and independent spirit.

Alec's passion for big cats found its ultimate expression in the Ol Jogi Wildlife Conservancy, a sprawling 66,000-acre estate in Kenya. The conservancy, originally acquired by the Wildenstein family, became a sanctuary for wildlife and a personal haven for Alec and Jocelyn.

Ol Jogi was home to a wide variety of animals, but the big cats were the crown jewels of the reserve. Lions, cheetahs, leopards, and other predators roamed the protected land, thriving under the care and conservation efforts spearheaded by Alec. He was deeply involved in the day-to-day operations of the conservancy, working closely with wildlife experts and veterinarians to ensure the animals' well-being.

The reserve's facilities reflected Alec's commitment to big cats. A state-of-the-art veterinary clinic was established on-site, equipped to handle the unique medical needs of the animals. Specialized enclosures and breeding programs were developed to support endangered species, contributing to global conservation efforts.

For Alec, big cats represented more than just wildlife; they symbolized power, grace, and a connection to the natural world that transcended human constructs. Their predatory instincts and commanding presence mirrored qualities Alec admired and perhaps saw in himself.

This personal connection extended to his aesthetic choices. The imagery of big cats featured prominently in the decor of his homes and estates. Sculptures, paintings, and even textiles depicting lions and leopards were common, blending his love for art with his admiration for these majestic creatures.

His fascination also influenced his relationship with Jocelyn. Alec's passion for big cats resonated with Jocelyn's own interest in exotic beauty and nature, creating a shared bond that deepened their connection. Jocelyn's eventual transformation, which many interpreted as an attempt to emulate feline features, can be seen as a reflection of Alec's profound influence on her life and identity.

Alec's love for big cats extended beyond personal admiration; he was also an advocate for their conservation. His efforts at Ol Jogi were part of a broader commitment to protecting endangered species and preserving the delicate ecosystems they inhabited.

Under Alec's guidance, the conservancy became a model for sustainable wildlife management. He worked to combat poaching, a major threat to big cats in Africa, by funding anti-poaching patrols and implementing advanced security measures. Alec also collaborated with international conservation organizations, lending his resources and influence to initiatives aimed at protecting big cats worldwide.

His work had a significant impact, not only on the animals at Ol Jogi but also on global awareness of the challenges facing big cats in the wild. Alec's efforts helped to ensure that future generations could continue to marvel at these extraordinary creatures, leaving a lasting legacy in the world of conservation.

Alec's devotion to big cats was not without its challenges. Maintaining a private conservancy of Ol Jogi's scale required significant financial resources and meticulous management. The high costs of staffing, security, and animal care were a constant strain, even for someone of Alec's wealth.

Additionally, Alec's private ownership of such a vast estate and its exotic inhabitants sometimes drew criticism from conservationists who believed wildlife should be left entirely to nature. Others questioned the ethics of keeping animals in captivity, even within a conservancy dedicated to their well-being. Despite these challenges, Alec remained steadfast in his commitment to big cats, viewing them as both a responsibility and a privilege.

Alec's passion for big cats had a profound influence on Jocelyn and their family life. Jocelyn embraced the world of wildlife and conservation, spending extensive time at Ol Jogi and participating in the care of the animals. Her eventual cosmetic transformations, often likened to feline features, underscored how deeply Alec's love for big cats shaped their relationship and her identity. For their children, growing up surrounded by such majestic creatures provided a unique upbringing. They were exposed to the beauty and challenges of wildlife conservation, learning firsthand the importance of protecting endangered species.

Alec Wildenstein's love for big cats remains one of the most distinctive aspects of his life and legacy. Through his efforts at Ol Jogi and his dedication to their preservation, Alec not only celebrated the beauty and majesty of these creatures but also contribute meaningfully to their survival.

His passion for big cats was a reflection of his character, bold, powerful, and unyielding. While his life was marked by privilege and controversy, his work with wildlife stands as a testament to his commitment to something greater than himself, ensuring that the majestic presence of big cats endures in the world for generations to come.

5.2 Jocelyn's Fascination with Feline Features

Jocelyn Wildenstein's fascination with feline features is one of the most iconic and controversial aspects of her public identity. Often dubbed "The Catwoman" by the media, Jocelyn's dramatic cosmetic transformations, inspired by the elegant and exotic beauty of big cats, have been the subject of endless debate, curiosity, and criticism. However, her interest in feline features was not just an aesthetic choice; it reflected deeper layers of her personality, passions, and even her relationships.

Jocelyn's love for feline beauty reportedly took root during her years with Alec Wildenstein, a man renowned for his devotion to big cats. Living at the Ol Jogi

Wildlife Conservancy in Kenya, she was surrounded by lions, leopards, and cheetahs, creatures whose power and grace left an indelible mark on her. These animals symbolize strength, mystery, and freedom, qualities Jocelyn admired and sought to embody in her own life.

The allure of feline features, with their sharp cheekbones, almond-shaped eyes, and sleek physicality, seemed to captivate Jocelyn. Over time, this admiration evolved into a desire to transform herself into a living embodiment of the qualities she revered in these majestic animals.

Jocelyn's decision to undergo extensive cosmetic surgery to emulate feline features was bold and groundbreaking, albeit polarizing. Beginning in the 1980s, she embarked on a series of procedures designed to enhance her cheekbones, elongate her eyes, and refine her jawline, features she associated with the big cats she loved.

The surgeries were dramatic and unorthodox, garnering both fascination and ridicule from the public. For

Jocelyn, however, the transformations were less about societal approval and more about personal expression. She viewed her face as a canvas, a work of art she could mold and shape to reflect her unique vision of beauty.

Alec played a significant role in Jocelyn's fascination with feline features. Reports suggest that he admired big cats deeply and encouraged Jocelyn's transformations to align with his aesthetic preferences. This dynamic added a layer of complexity to her choices, blending personal desire with the influence of her partner. Jocelyn's transformation can also be seen as a testament to her devotion to Alec and their shared passion for wildlife, particularly big cats. Her evolving appearance became a physical manifestation of their bond and their life together at Ol Jogi.

For Jocelyn, feline beauty symbolized much more than physical allure. It represented qualities she sought to embody in her own life:

Strength and Power: Big cats are apex predators, commanding respect and fear in their natural habitats. Jocelyn's transformation reflected her desire to project strength and independence, especially as a woman navigating the upper echelons of society.

Mystery and Allure: Cats are often associated with mystique and sensuality. Jocelyn's feline-inspired features mirrored this enigmatic quality, setting her apart from traditional standards of beauty.

Exoticism: Felines, particularly leopards and lions, are often seen as exotic creatures. Jocelyn's appearance reflected her fascination with the rare and extraordinary, aligning with her broader aesthetic tastes in art, fashion, and lifestyle.

Jocelyn's transformations sparked intense public interest and media scrutiny. Dubbed "The Bride of Wildenstein" and "Catwoman," her appearance became a topic of endless debate. Critics labeled her as an example of cosmetic surgery gone too far, while others admired her audacity and commitment to personal expression.

Despite the criticism, Jocelyn remained unapologetic about her choices. She rejected societal norms of beauty and embraced her own vision, challenging traditional expectations and sparking conversations about body autonomy and self-expression. Her resilience in the face of ridicule highlighted her strength and confidence, traits she likely associated with the feline creatures she admired.

While Jocelyn's fascination with feline features was largely aesthetic, it also hinted at deeper emotional and psychological layers. Her transformation can be seen as a coping mechanism during tumultuous periods in her life, including her divorce from Alec and the intense media attention that followed. In a world that often sought to define and constrain her, Jocelyn's decision to transform herself was an act of defiance and self-assertion. It was her way of taking control of her identity and rewriting the narrative about who she was and what she represented.

Jocelyn's feline-inspired features have left an indelible mark on pop culture and discussions around beauty standards. While her appearance was polarizing, it challenged the notion that beauty must conform to conventional norms. Jocelyn's story became a symbol of how far people are willing to go in pursuit of their ideal selves, raising questions about the limits of self-expression and the role of society in shaping perceptions of beauty.

Her influence extended to fashion, art, and entertainment, where feline-inspired aesthetics became a recurring theme. From runway looks to editorial photography, Jocelyn's unique vision of beauty resonated in unexpected ways, inspiring a new appreciation for bold and unconventional styles.

Jocelyn Wildenstein's fascination with feline features is a testament to her individuality and creativity. While her choices were often misunderstood, they reflected a deep connection to the qualities she admired in big cats and a fearless commitment to living life on her terms.

Her transformation, though controversial, has sparked conversations about beauty, art, and identity that continue to resonate. Jocelyn's story reminds us that beauty is subjective, and the pursuit of one's ideal self, no matter how unconventional, is a deeply personal journey deserving of respect and understanding.

CHAPTER SIX: THE FIRST CUT

The decision to alter one's physical appearance, especially through cosmetic surgery, is always deeply personal. For Jocelyn Wildenstein, "the first cut" marked the beginning of a transformative journey that would come to define much of her life and public image. It was a moment that merged personal ambition, external influences, and a fascination with the idea of beauty as a form of self-expression. This initial step was not just a physical transformation but also a psychological and emotional turning point.

Before undergoing her first cosmetic procedure, Jocelyn Wildenstein lived a life already marked by opulence and drama. Married to Alec Wildenstein, heir to a multi-billion-dollar art empire, Jocelyn's world was one of wealth, luxury, and high society. However, behind the glamour, her marriage was fraught with tension and challenges, including rumors of infidelity and emotional distance.

During this period, Jocelyn's fascination with exotic beauty, particularly feline features, began to take shape. Inspired by her husband's love for big cats and her time spent at the Ol Jogi Wildlife Conservancy in Kenya, Jocelyn grew enamored with the elegance, mystery, and power these creatures represented.

The decision to undergo cosmetic surgery was driven by a combination of personal desire and external circumstances. Jocelyn reportedly believed that enhancing her appearance would reignite the passion in her marriage and align her physical image with the feline beauty she admired.

It's said that Alec himself encouraged Jocelyn's initial steps toward transformation, further influencing her decision. Whether motivated by his preferences or her own fascination, Jocelyn saw cosmetic surgery as a way to embody the qualities she revered in big cats, grace, strength, and allure.

While the exact details of Jocelyn's first cosmetic procedure remain somewhat speculative, it is widely believed that her journey began with subtle enhancements. These initial steps likely involved procedures such as cheekbone augmentation or eyelid surgery, designed to create the high cheekbones and almond-shaped eyes reminiscent of feline features.

At the time, cosmetic surgery was still emerging as a mainstream practice, particularly among the elite. Jocelyn's willingness to embrace these procedures reflected her boldness and readiness to experiment with her appearance, even in the face of potential risks and societal judgment. The first cut was not merely a physical alteration but also an emotional and psychological milestone. Jocelyn's transformation gave her a sense of control over her identity and allowed her to channel her fascination with beauty into a tangible form.

However, it also opened the door to new challenges. The changes to her appearance, though initially subtle, attracted attention from those around her. Friends, family, and members of high society began to notice her evolving look, sparking curiosity and, in some cases, criticism. For Jocelyn, these reactions were a double-edged sword. On one hand, she relished the newfound sense of empowerment and individuality her transformation brought. On the other hand, the scrutiny foreshadowed the intense public fascination and judgment that would later define her life.

The first cut was just the beginning. The satisfaction Jocelyn derived from her initial transformation encouraged her to pursue further procedures. With each step, she moved closer to her vision of beauty, becoming more daring and experimental in her choices. This process of continual enhancement became a defining aspect of Jocelyn's identity. She viewed her physical transformation as an ongoing work of art, one that required constant refinement and evolution.

Even in its early stages, Jocelyn's transformation elicited mixed reactions. Among her inner circle, there were those who admired her boldness and commitment to self-expression, while others questioned the necessity and motivation behind the changes.

Privately, Jocelyn grappled with the complexities of her journey. While she found empowerment in her ability to reshape her appearance, she also faced the emotional toll of societal expectations and her own pursuit of perfection. The first cut set a precedent for Jocelyn's life, intertwining her physical transformation with her personal struggles, relationships, and public image.

In hindsight, the first cut was more than just a surgical procedure, it was a turning point that redefined Jocelyn's relationship with beauty, identity, and the world around her. It marked the beginning of her journey as a figure who challenged conventional notions of aesthetics and sparked conversations about the limits of self-expression.

For Jocelyn, the decision to undergo that initial procedure was an act of courage and creativity. It was the first step toward becoming the person she envisioned, one who embodied the grace and mystery of the feline creatures she so admired.

The first cut laid the foundation for Jocelyn's lifelong transformation, shaping her into a polarizing and unforgettable figure. While her journey has been met with both admiration and criticism, it remains a testament to her determination to live authentically and unapologetically. Ultimately, the first cut was not just a change in Jocelyn's appearance, it was a declaration of her commitment to self-expression, individuality, and the pursuit of a beauty that resonated deeply with her soul.

6.1 Jocelyn's Foray into Cosmetic Surgery

Jocelyn Wildenstein's journey into the world of cosmetic surgery is one of the most well-known yet misunderstood aspects of her life. Her dramatic transformation became a defining feature of her identity and a frequent topic of public fascination and media scrutiny.

However, beneath the headlines and caricatures lies a nuanced story of personal ambition, emotional vulnerability, and a desire for self-expression. Jocelyn's foray into cosmetic surgery was not just a series of medical procedures, it was a deeply personal journey shaped by her relationships, lifestyle, and unique vision of beauty.

Jocelyn's initial interest in cosmetic surgery stemmed from a combination of personal and external influences. Married to Alec Wildenstein, an art dealer and billionaire heir, Jocelyn lived a life immersed in luxury and high society. However, the pressures of maintaining a public image and the emotional challenges within her marriage pushed her toward self-reinvention.

Jocelyn's fascination with feline beauty played a pivotal role in her decision to undergo surgery. Inspired by the exotic allure of big cats, particularly those she encountered at Ol Jogi Wildlife Conservancy, she sought to embody their strength, elegance, and mystique. Additionally, Alec's admiration for feline aesthetics reportedly encouraged her transformation, as she aimed to align her appearance with his preferences and her own growing aesthetic ideals.

Jocelyn's journey began with subtle procedures aimed at enhancing specific features. These initial surgeries included:

Cheekbone Augmentation: High cheekbones were one of Jocelyn's primary aesthetic goals, inspired by the sharp, defined facial structure of big cats.

Blepharoplasty (Eyelid Surgery): To achieve an almond-shaped, feline-like gaze, Jocelyn underwent procedures to reshape her eyes.

Lip Enhancement: Fuller lips were another aspect of her transformation, reflecting the sensuality often associated with feline beauty.

At the time, cosmetic surgery was becoming more accessible to the wealthy elite but remained controversial and shrouded in secrecy. Jocelyn's willingness to embrace it reflected her boldness and commitment to personal reinvention.

What began as minor enhancements soon evolved into a more comprehensive and ongoing transformation. Over the years, Jocelyn underwent numerous procedures, each building upon the last, to further refine her appearance. These included:

Facelifts: To maintain a youthful and sculpted appearance.

Dermal Fillers and Implants: Used to add volume and definition to her facial structure.

Chin and Jawline Reshaping: To achieve the sleek, elongated features reminiscent of big cats.

Her transformation was not static; it was a continuous process, reflecting her evolving vision of beauty. Jocelyn viewed her face as a canvas, an artwork that required constant refinement to achieve perfection.

Jocelyn's foray into cosmetic surgery was deeply intertwined with her emotional and psychological journey. At its core, her transformation was a response to both internal desires and external pressures.

Personal Empowerment: Jocelyn saw her surgeries as a way to take control of her appearance and identity, defying societal norms and expectations.

Relationship Dynamics: Her marriage to Alec Wildenstein played a significant role in shaping her decisions. Some accounts suggest she underwent surgeries to rekindle Alec's affection and align with his preferences, while others emphasize her independent pursuit of an aesthetic vision.

Coping Mechanism: Cosmetic surgery became a way for Jocelyn to navigate the emotional challenges of her life, including marital strife, public scrutiny, and a sense of alienation from traditional beauty standards.

As Jocelyn's transformation became more pronounced, it drew widespread attention from the media and the public. Dubbed "The Bride of Wildenstein" and "Catwoman," her appearance became a subject of fascination, ridicule, and debate.

Criticism: Many viewed her transformation as excessive, labeling her as an example of the dangers of cosmetic surgery addiction.

Admiration: Others admired her courage to embrace a unique and unconventional vision of beauty, challenging societal norms.

Curiosity: Jocelyn's story sparked conversations about the psychological and emotional dimensions of cosmetic surgery, as well as its role in modern beauty culture.

Despite the scrutiny, Jocelyn remained unapologetic about her choices, emphasizing her right to define her own identity and pursue the aesthetic ideals that resonated with her.

Jocelyn's foray into cosmetic surgery has had a lasting impact on discussions around beauty, identity, and self-expression.

Challenging Norms: Her transformation challenged traditional standards of beauty, highlighting the subjective and evolving nature of aesthetic ideals.

Body Autonomy: Jocelyn's story underscored the importance of personal choice in matters of appearance, even in the face of societal judgment.

Cultural Conversations: Her journey contributed to broader discussions about the role of cosmetic surgery in modern society, particularly its psychological and emotional implications.

Jocelyn Wildenstein's foray into cosmetic surgery is a testament to her individuality, creativity, and resilience. While her choices were often misunderstood and criticized, they reflected a deeply personal journey of self-expression and reinvention.

Her story serves as a reminder that beauty is subjective and that the pursuit of one's ideal self is a deeply personal endeavor. For Jocelyn, cosmetic surgery was not just about altering her appearance, it was about embracing her passions, asserting her identity, and defying the limitations imposed by societal norms. In doing so, she became a symbol of both the power and the complexity of self-expression in the modern world.

6.2 Balancing Societal Expectations and Personal Desires

Jocelyn Wildenstein's life story is marked by a constant tug-of-war between the expectations placed on her by society and her own personal desires. This delicate balance, or at times, the struggle to maintain it, defined much of her public and private life. From her lavish lifestyle and cosmetic transformations to her relationships and personal reinvention, Jocelyn navigated a complex web of societal norms, gender expectations, and her own personal vision. Her experiences reflect broader themes of identity, body autonomy, and the pressures faced by women in the public eye.

Jocelyn Wildenstein was born into a world that placed a high premium on beauty, wealth, and social standing. Her entry into high society came with its own set of expectations, many of which revolved around maintaining an image of perfection, grace, and class. As a young woman in the 1970s and 1980s, Jocelyn was thrust into a world of elite New York socialites, fashion icons, and art patrons, environments that were, at times, unforgiving.

At a fundamental level, societal expectations around beauty for women, particularly women in the public eye, dictated that they must embody traditional notions of femininity, often related to youth, smooth skin, and idealized proportions. Jocelyn was not immune to this pressure. As she became more deeply embedded in her role as Alec Wildenstein's wife and a figure in the world of high society, the standard of beauty and elegance she had to meet grew more rigid.

Jocelyn's marriage to Alec Wildenstein, a man whose family was renowned for its vast wealth and involvement in the world of fine art, raised her status significantly. In this new echelon of wealth, social life was defined by appearances, fabulous parties, private jet travel, luxury vacations, and art collections. She was expected to present herself as a flawless and desirable partner who was as much a part of Alec's art empire as the priceless paintings he collected.

Her beauty became her most valued asset in this world, and she was expected to maintain an image of youthful vitality. As time passed and signs of aging began to show, the pressure to stay young and perfect grew. This external pressure to conform to an almost unattainable beauty ideal pushed Jocelyn toward cosmetic surgery.

Her journey into self-reinvention, with its various procedures, represented a direct response to the growing expectations placed on her by society. However, each step she took toward altering her appearance reflected a deeper internal struggle, not only to please those around her but also to maintain control over her self-image.

Jocelyn's desire to transform her physical appearance through surgery cannot solely be attributed to societal pressures. Beneath the surface, her journey into cosmetic enhancement was also motivated by a need to express herself in ways that aligned with her personal aesthetic. She had a vision of beauty that was unique to her: inspired by the power and grace of big cats, an image she associated with freedom, sensuality, and exotic allure.

Her personal desires were closely intertwined with her identity and self-worth. Her cosmetic procedures became a form of artistic self-expression, an attempt to physically embody the characteristics of the creatures she admired. For Jocelyn, these transformations were less about appeasing others and more about defining herself on her own terms, although this quest was often complicated by the world's gaze upon her.

It's crucial to understand that for Jocelyn, this personal aesthetic was not a whim but rather a profound part of her identity. The pursuit of beauty for her was not about conforming to a universal standard but about reflecting her inner vision of perfection, a concept heavily influenced by her love for nature, exoticism, and the mysterious allure of the feline form. In this way, her desire to alter her appearance became as much an act of self-discovery as it was an act of artistic creation.

Despite her deep personal conviction, Jocelyn's quest for beauty and self-expression was continuously met with public scrutiny. Her cosmetic surgeries became a topic of fascination for the media, with outlets branding her as "The Catwoman" or "The Bride of Wildenstein." The intense media coverage she received often focused on the physical aspects of her transformation, overshadowing her more profound motivations.

This kind of public attention often had the effect of reinforcing societal expectations, constantly reminding her that she was being judged not just for her beauty, but for her ability to fit into the idealized mold of a wealthy, glamorous woman. As a result, Jocelyn became trapped in a cycle: every surgical enhancement, every public appearance, was another effort to meet the ever-shifting standards of beauty, while simultaneously trying to meet her own desire for uniqueness and freedom.

At times, this scrutiny took a toll on her. The constant media coverage of her surgeries, relationships, and personal life fostered a sense of objectification. Her identity became increasingly entwined with the image the media had constructed for her. In the eyes of the public, she was no longer just Jocelyn Wildenstein, but a living symbol of excess, vanity, and the cost of fame. Yet, despite this, Jocelyn continued her journey of self-reinvention, driven by her desire to live authentically, even if it was at odds with societal views.

As a woman of immense wealth and beauty, Jocelyn was also bound by the gendered expectations of her time. In many ways, society expected her to uphold traditional roles as a wife, mother, and hostess, all while maintaining an image of flawless femininity. For Jocelyn, being in the public eye meant that her worth was often reduced to her appearance and her ability to maintain an idealized role as a wealthy woman of beauty.

The pressure to maintain this ideal femininity, especially as she aged, exacerbated her feelings of insecurity and influenced her decision to undergo extensive cosmetic procedures. While many of her male counterparts, including her husband Alec, were allowed to age without facing similar scrutiny, Jocelyn's beauty and youthfulness were constantly measured against the ideal image of the perfect, ageless woman. Her pursuit of a feline-inspired appearance was in many ways a response to this dual burden, fighting against both societal expectations and the pressures that come with being a public figure.

Ultimately, Jocelyn's story highlights the complexity of balancing societal expectations with personal desires. While she navigated the glamorous world of high society, Jocelyn never fully conformed to the norms set by those around her. Her cosmetic surgeries, driven by a unique aesthetic vision, became her way of both defying and responding to the rigid beauty standards imposed on her. However, her journey also shows how, at times, the quest for personal authenticity can be overshadowed by the need to conform to the expectations of the world.

Jocelyn Wildenstein's life underscores the powerful influence of societal pressures, particularly on women, but also the strength it takes to pursue one's own vision of identity, even when faced with intense criticism and public scrutiny. Her story is one of resilience in the face of societal judgment, as well as an ongoing quest to align her personal desires with the complex web of expectations placed on her by both the world around her and her own internal standards of beauty.

CHAPTER SEVEN: THE MEDIA FRENZY

The life of Jocelyn Wildenstein has been inseparable from the constant media attention that began in the 1990s and continues to this day. This public scrutiny, particularly surrounding her extensive cosmetic transformations, created an unrelenting media frenzy that magnified every aspect of her existence, often reducing her to a caricature of excess and vanity. From the moment her appearance began to evolve through cosmetic surgeries, Jocelyn found herself thrust into the spotlight, her personal journey of self-transformation becoming a subject of tabloid fascination and public judgment.

The media frenzy surrounding Jocelyn Wildenstein's transformation began in earnest after she underwent a series of cosmetic surgeries that drastically altered her facial features. Her decision to undergo multiple procedures, particularly those that seemed to emulate feline characteristics, was a visual change that the media seized upon. Jocelyn's appearance, with its high cheekbones, sculpted jawline, and almond-shaped eyes, became the focal point of many articles, news stories, and photoshoots.

While Jocelyn had been a fixture in high society for years due to her marriage to Alec Wildenstein, it was the dramatic changes to her appearance that turned her into a media sensation. Tabloids and gossip columns, which thrive on sensationalism and scandal, found a goldmine in Jocelyn's metamorphosis. Her transformation was not only extraordinary but seemingly defied conventional beauty standards. This gave the media a reason to frame her story in provocative ways, often emphasizing the perceived excesses of her procedures.

As Jocelyn's appearance evolved, the press began to tag her with various nicknames, some cruel and others highlighting her increasingly feline-like features. Terms like "Catwoman," "The Bride of Wildenstein," and "The $4 million face" became shorthand for her transformation. The media didn't just focus on the physical changes but also delved into her relationship with Alec Wildenstein, a rich and reclusive art heir.

The juxtaposition of her extravagant lifestyle and her unusual appearance led to a flurry of headlines that were more focused on spectacle than substance. Her cosmetic surgeries were presented as a form of vanity, and her personal choices were often reduced to the stereotypical narrative of a woman desperately trying to maintain youth and beauty for the sake of her marriage. It's important to note that much of the media's portrayal of Jocelyn was shaped by preconceptions of femininity, aging, and wealth, with her surgeries often framed as an example of excess, obsession, and self-doubt.

This kind of tabloid treatment further objectified Jocelyn. Her appearance became the centerpiece of a story that placed her as an example of everything wrong with a society obsessed with beauty, youth, and the pursuit of perfection. However, this portrayal obscured the more complex motivations behind her decisions, such as her passion for beauty and art, as well as her deep personal fascination with feline aesthetics.

Jocelyn's transformation was exaggerated in the media, which focused on the more extreme aspects of her surgeries. Her appearance was depicted as being abnormal or grotesque, while the reality of her personal motivations for the procedures was largely ignored. The framing of Jocelyn as a tragic figure whose surgeries spiraled out of control created a narrative of cautionary excess.

The media had a particular tendency to sensationalize the physical aspects of her surgeries, often featuring before-and-after pictures and pointing out the most dramatic elements of her appearance. In a society where cosmetic surgery was increasingly common, Jocelyn became a symbol of the extremes to which some would go in the pursuit of beauty. This created an oversimplified and distorted public perception of her, overshadowing her identity and reducing her to a "freak show" spectacle.

The media's interest in Jocelyn Wildenstein wasn't limited to her physical transformation. Her high-profile marriage to Alec Wildenstein, which ended in a bitter divorce, was another fuel for the media frenzy. Alec, heir to an immense fortune tied to the family's art empire, was a recluse who preferred to stay out of the limelight, adding an element of mystery to their relationship.

Their marriage, filled with rumors of infidelity, was widely covered in the media. Some outlets speculated that Jocelyn's surgeries were driven by an attempt to regain Alec's affection, reinforcing the narrative that her transformation was born from insecurity and the need to hold onto a marriage that was clearly in turmoil. This speculation only intensified after their divorce in 1999, which saw Jocelyn fight for a portion of Alec's wealth.

The media played a key role in framing this divorce as a dramatic and scandalous event, with stories emphasizing the "battle" over money and the infamous photos of Jocelyn with her new appearance. Alec's fortune and their lavish lifestyle provided a perfect backdrop for the story, further fueling public interest. Jocelyn was depicted as a woman whose obsession with beauty and wealth had led her down a dangerous path, one of cosmetic surgery and marital discord.

Over the years, the media's portrayal of Jocelyn Wildenstein became a defining part of her public identity. While she had once been a wealthy socialite who mingled with the elite, she was now seen by many as a tragic figure whose pursuit of beauty led to her ultimate undoing.

The constant scrutiny of her appearance took a significant emotional toll. The ridicule, mockery, and obsession with her looks must have been difficult for Jocelyn, especially considering that her decision to undergo surgery was fueled by personal desires, not just to fulfill societal standards of beauty.

As time went on, the media continued to focus on her physical appearance, emphasizing her aging process and the seemingly "unnatural" results of her surgeries. These depictions were often out of context, ignoring the deeper aspects of her journey and reducing her to a one-dimensional figure. Despite this, Jocelyn remained defiant in her personal choices. She continued to embrace her transformation, refusing to be defined by the media's reductive portrayals.

Jocelyn Wildenstein's media coverage is an example of the power the press has in shaping and influencing public perceptions of individuals, especially women. Her story is emblematic of the objectification women often face in the media, where the focus is placed more on appearance and public personas than on the complexities of their experiences and inner lives. The media frenzy surrounding Jocelyn reflects the broader cultural issues of body image, aging, and gender expectations, all of which are often tied to a person's worth in the public eye.

In the case of Jocelyn, the media obsession with her surgeries became a lens through which larger discussions of beauty, vanity, and personal autonomy were filtered. The intense scrutiny ultimately led to a reduction of her identity to her physical transformation, while her personal motivations and the emotional intricacies of her life remained largely ignored. The media frenzy she experienced highlights the dangers of this kind of public treatment, where the individuality of a person is sacrificed for entertainment, sensationalism, and scandal.

The media frenzy surrounding Jocelyn Wildenstein was not just about her appearance, it was about the perception of beauty, femininity, and wealth in society. It was about how a woman who defied traditional norms became an object of public fascination and ridicule.

Over time, Jocelyn became a symbol of the dangers of vanity and excess, but also of the power of self-expression. Despite the intense media coverage and the mockery she faced, Jocelyn's story remains one of complexity and resilience, highlighting the human desire for reinvention and identity in the face of external pressures.

Through the lens of the media frenzy, we see how public perception is shaped, how the private lives of individuals become entertainment fodder, and how the pursuit of personal desires can sometimes be misinterpreted, misunderstood, or distorted by external forces. For Jocelyn Wildenstein, the media frenzy became inescapable, but it also served to cement her place in pop culture as one of the most talked-about figures of the 21st century.

7.1 Public Reactions to Her Evolving Appearance

The public's reaction to Jocelyn Wildenstein's evolving appearance stands as one of the most striking aspects of her life and public persona. As she underwent a series of surgeries to transform her face, she became the subject of intense scrutiny, fascination, and judgment.

The media, alongside public opinion, reacted in ways that were sometimes harsh, often sensational, and occasionally even sympathetic. These reactions were multifaceted and layered, driven by cultural norms around beauty, aging, and gender, as well as the sheer shock value of her physical transformation.

When Jocelyn Wildenstein first began to alter her appearance with cosmetic procedures, the public reaction was a mixture of curiosity and intrigue. The early stages of her transformation did not elicit as strong a reaction as later developments did, but it was clear that she had become a figure to watch. The world was slowly introduced to her new look through rare photos and public appearances.

At this point, some members of the public were simply fascinated by the changes she was making. Her increasingly feline-like features caught the eye of those who followed celebrity gossip and socialite culture. The idea of altering one's appearance for aesthetic reasons was not unheard of, but Jocelyn's choices were seen as more dramatic and far-reaching than most. The media was quick to label her transformation as unusual and extreme, but at this stage, the focus was more on her wealth, social standing, and her marriage to Alec Wildenstein than on her surgeries.

For those who admired Jocelyn's extravagant lifestyle, her evolving appearance became part of her mystique. Her appearance was seen as a reflection of her lavishness and desire to transcend traditional beauty standards. In this way, there was an early curiosity about how far she would take her transformations, with some seeing her as a symbol of boldness and defiance against age and conventional beauty.

As Jocelyn's appearance continued to evolve, her facial features began to take on more dramatic and pronounced feline characteristics. The press seized on this shift, drawing comparisons between her increasingly exotic look and that of a cat. By the time her facial changes became more extreme, the public's reaction had shifted from fascination to outright shock.

Her appearance, marked by high, angular cheekbones, exaggerated eyelids, and a taut, almost sculpted jawline, was widely covered by tabloids. Her new look was perceived as so extraordinary that it became fodder for jokes, ridicule, and mockery. Headlines like "Catwoman" and "The Bride of Wildenstein" became ubiquitous, as the press and public latched onto her transformation, reducing her to a figure of spectacle. What had once been seen as a private journey into self-expression became a source of public amusement.

The public, especially those who did not know her personally, reacted harshly. Many criticized her for "ruining" her natural beauty, questioning why someone would go to such extreme lengths to alter their appearance. The sheer shock value of her look often overshadowed the reality of her motivations. Jocelyn, who had undergone surgery to fulfill her personal aesthetic desires, was now a target for societal judgment, judgment that was based on narrow definitions of beauty and aging.

With the rise of social media in the late 2000s and beyond, public reactions to Jocelyn's appearance became even more widespread and instantaneous. Social media platforms like Twitter, Instagram, and Facebook allowed individuals to react to her photos with greater immediacy, and the anonymity of online interactions emboldened harsh comments and criticisms. The narrative around Jocelyn's appearance took on a life of its own, often being reduced to a "freak show" or "cautionary tale" about the dangers of vanity and cosmetic surgery.

On the internet, memes and jokes about her appearance flourished, and the public turned her into a punchline. The depersonalization of Jocelyn, as someone who had chosen to alter her appearance in ways that defied traditional beauty norms, led to the widespread ridicule of her face. People often focused on the most dramatic aspects of her appearance, the high cheekbones, the wide eyes, the thin lips, rather than understanding the complex reasons behind her surgeries.

This online culture of mocking and memeification is emblematic of society's broader tendency to reduce people to stereotypes, often ignoring the deeper motivations or struggles behind their decisions. In Jocelyn's case, her personal desires to create an appearance that aligned with her love of exotic animals and her own sense of beauty were overshadowed by public perceptions of her as a victim of cosmetic excess.

Amidst the widespread ridicule and condemnation, there were also individuals who empathized with Jocelyn and expressed sympathy for the judgment she faced. Some viewed her transformation as a reflection of a woman's agency and autonomy over her own body. These supporters argued that Jocelyn had every right to express herself in whatever way she chose, and that her choices should not be reduced to ridicule.

Additionally, some commentators and individuals from the world of art and beauty saw Jocelyn's transformations as an attempt at self-expression, a creative and artistic endeavor. As someone who lived in the world of high art, it was not entirely out of character for Jocelyn to view her body as a canvas. For these supporters, Jocelyn's choices were seen as bold and artistic rather than grotesque. However, this sympathetic narrative rarely gained mainstream traction.

Some saw the cruelty and mockery she faced as rooted in broader societal issues, including ageism, sexism, and classism. As a wealthy woman who chose to undergo cosmetic surgery to maintain her beauty, Jocelyn was often seen as a symbol of excess and privilege, making her a target for societal resentment. In a culture that often feels uncomfortable with the idea of women taking control of their own bodies, Jocelyn's extreme transformation triggered conversations about gender expectations and the lengths women are sometimes pushed to in order to maintain relevance in a youth-obsessed culture.

The reactions to Jocelyn Wildenstein's evolving appearance can also be viewed through the lens of gender expectations and societal views on aging. As a woman, Jocelyn faced an immense amount of scrutiny for her decision to undergo cosmetic surgery, something that would have likely been more accepted or less noticed had she been a man. The pressure for women to maintain youthful, "perfect" appearances is a societal issue that has been exacerbated by the media's portrayal of aging, particularly in women of wealth and fame.

The media's obsession with Jocelyn's appearance became an extension of this larger cultural conversation about aging and beauty. Aging women, particularly those in the public eye, are often punished for the natural process of getting older. In Jocelyn's case, her extreme surgeries were viewed as an attempt to stave off the inevitable effects of aging, which made her a figure of both fascination and distaste.

By transforming her face, Jocelyn challenged the conventional narrative that women must age gracefully and naturally. Her surgeries were often interpreted as an act of defiance against the aging process, and as such, the public and media responses were steeped in judgment and often cruelty.

Public opinion on Jocelyn's appearance has always been highly polarized. For some, she was a cautionary tale, a woman who had gone too far, losing sight of her natural beauty in an attempt to chase an unattainable ideal. For others, she was a victim of societal pressures, a woman who faced intense scrutiny and judgment simply for choosing to alter her appearance in a way that suited her personal desires.

While Jocelyn herself never seemed to back down from her choices, the world around her continued to judge, celebrate, or mock her based on how her appearance deviated from accepted norms. The polarized nature of public opinion reflected society's broader discomfort with those who defy traditional ideas of beauty, age, and gender. In a world where conformity is often expected, Jocelyn's extreme transformation made her a symbol of rebellion, but also one of vulnerability.

Jocelyn Wildenstein's evolving appearance was not just a matter of physical change, it was a flashpoint for societal debates about beauty, aging, gender, and the pressures faced by women in the public eye. Public reactions to her transformation were varied, ranging from ridicule to sympathy, and they highlighted the tension between personal agency and societal expectations.

Ultimately, Jocelyn's appearance became an emblem of the complex and sometimes contradictory ways in which society judges individuals based on their outward appearance. Her journey reflects the deep-seated cultural anxieties around aging and beauty, as well as the challenges that women in particular face when their personal choices, especially regarding appearance, are scrutinized and dissected by the public.

7.2 The Rise of the "Catwoman" Moniker

The term "Catwoman" became synonymous with Jocelyn Wildenstein as the media fixated on her increasingly feline-like appearance, particularly in the late 1990s and early 2000s. Her physical transformation, fueled by a series of cosmetic surgeries, ignited a media frenzy, and it was during this time that the nickname "Catwoman" emerged. The term, rooted in a popular cultural reference, quickly became a defining and enduring label, shaping Jocelyn's public identity for years to come.

However, the rise of this moniker was not just about the physical changes to her face, but also about the way the media and public interpreted her decision to alter her appearance. The "Catwoman" tag represented a confluence of cultural, aesthetic, and gendered issues that framed Jocelyn's life in the public eye in a way that often overshadowed her personal motivations.

Jocelyn's transformation began as a personal pursuit, an attempt to reshape her appearance, but as her surgeries became more extreme, the media took notice. The dramatic changes to her facial structure, especially the alteration of her eyes, cheekbones, and jawline, started to resemble the features of a cat. Her elongated eyelids and prominent cheekbones gave her a distinctly exotic look, one that seemed to mirror the feline aesthetic that would later become her hallmark in the eyes of the press.

As this transformation became more noticeable, the tabloids and media outlets began to describe Jocelyn in increasingly sensational terms. What might have been a private, personal decision soon became the subject of intense public fascination and ridicule. It was the tabloids, in particular, that seized upon the idea of Jocelyn resembling a cat, drawing comparisons to the fictional "Catwoman," a popular comic book character known for her feline traits and seductive allure.

By the time Jocelyn's appearance had undergone multiple procedures, the media had dubbed her "Catwoman." This nickname was not simply a reflection of her changing appearance but was also a way to further sensationalize her story. The press found that using a well-known cultural reference allowed them to instantly communicate a sense of intrigue and exoticism, linking

Jocelyn's physical transformation to a larger narrative of beauty, power, and mystery.

The "Catwoman" moniker quickly took on a life of its own, becoming a shorthand for her altered appearance and the scandal surrounding her surgeries. It was a nickname that stuck, even as Jocelyn herself seemed to resent being defined by it. But in the world of tabloids, a catchy, provocative nickname was a powerful tool for creating a persona, and the media's fascination with her new look meant that the "Catwoman" label became inescapable.

The popularity of the "Catwoman" nickname also played into broader cultural themes. The character of Catwoman, first introduced in the 1940s as a cat burglar with a complex, seductive persona, had long been associated with femininity, mystery, and allure. She was a strong, independent woman who, despite being a villain, often commanded admiration for her intelligence, beauty, and ability to bend the rules. In the 1990s, particularly with Michelle Pfeiffer's portrayal in Batman

Returns (1992), Catwoman had a resurgence in pop culture, embodying a darker, more complex side of female empowerment and sexuality.

The media's use of this nickname aligned Jocelyn with these iconic themes, casting her as a woman who had taken control of her own body and appearance in a bold and controversial way. The comparison to Catwoman worked on a symbolic level, it suggested that Jocelyn had become a creature of transformation, capable of reinvention, just as Catwoman could change between her civilian identity and her mysterious alter-ego.

However, the media's interpretation of Jocelyn as a "Catwoman" figure was far less empowering. Instead of celebrating her for challenging societal beauty standards, the media often ridiculed her decision to alter her appearance, reducing her to a spectacle of excess. While Catwoman was admired for her strength and independence, Jocelyn was largely viewed as a tragic figure who had gone too far in her pursuit of beauty.

The rise of the "Catwoman" moniker signified a shift in
public perception of Jocelyn Wildenstein. Initially, she
was a wealthy socialite and wife of art heir Alec
Wildenstein, known for her opulent lifestyle. But once
her appearance began to change, the media's focus
shifted dramatically toward her physical transformation,
and the "Catwoman" label became synonymous with her
identity in the public eye. The name, while instantly
recognizable, quickly took on a mocking tone, especially
as the surgeries became more pronounced and public.

The media turned Jocelyn's appearance into a spectacle,
something to be ogled and ridiculed. It wasn't long
before her transformation became the subject of harsh
jokes and criticisms, with some outlets using the
"Catwoman" label to emphasize the extremes of her
surgery, portraying her as someone who had lost control
of her own vanity.

This shift from fascination to ridicule highlights the
broader societal tendency to punish individuals,
particularly women, who break away from conventional

standards of beauty or who take extreme measures to alter their appearance. While her cosmetic procedures were a personal decision, the public and media's reaction framed them as excessive, and by using the "Catwoman" nickname, they reduced her complex story to a punchline.

Jocelyn Wildenstein's response to the "Catwoman" moniker was one of defiance. She never seemed to embrace the nickname, but she did refuse to be silenced by the media's ridicule. In interviews, Jocelyn explained that her surgeries were not done to satisfy the public but rather to fulfill her own vision of beauty. She had a deep personal connection to the feline features she sought to achieve, inspired by her love for cats and her admiration for the grace and strength they symbolized.

Despite the negative attention, Jocelyn never publicly regretted her decisions. In interviews, she stood by her choices, asserting that the surgeries were a form of personal expression and a reflection of her love for beauty and art. She rejected the judgment cast upon her, refusing to allow the "Catwoman" nickname to define her entirely. In some ways, Jocelyn's defiance to the media's framing of her identity can be seen as an act of strength, as she maintained control over her narrative in a world that tried to reduce her to a spectacle.

However, the "Catwoman" label persisted, especially in the tabloid culture, where sensationalized stories thrive. The nickname became a permanent part of her legacy, one that overshadowed her deeper motivations and her multifaceted identity. It wasn't just her appearance that defined her in the eyes of the public, but the media's ability to distort her story into a sensational headline.

The "Catwoman" moniker, though often used derisively, became an indelible part of Jocelyn Wildenstein's public persona. In many ways, it served to encapsulate how the media and public view those who challenge conventional beauty standards or pursue extreme forms of self-transformation. It highlighted the way society tends to judge women based on their appearance and how public figures can be reduced to one-dimensional caricatures.

For Jocelyn, the "Catwoman" label became an emblem of both her personal journey and the media's tendency to distort individual stories. While it reflected her love for feline aesthetics, it also became shorthand for excess, vanity, and obsession. The nickname, though rooted in a reference to a popular comic book character, ultimately played into the tabloid-driven narrative of spectacle and scandal that defined much of Jocelyn's life in the public eye.

Despite the ridicule and negative press, Jocelyn's resilience in facing the "Catwoman" label showed her ability to maintain her sense of self. Whether viewed as a victim of her own vanity or as a symbol of radical self-expression, the rise of the "Catwoman" moniker ensured that Jocelyn Wildenstein's story would be one of the most talked-about and polarizing tales in celebrity culture. The nickname, while deeply tied to her physical transformation, also became a part of her larger legacy, one marked by both the power of self-reinvention and the dangers of being consumed by public opinion.

CHAPTER EIGHT: PERFECTION AT A PRICE

The concept of "perfection" has long been a driving force in human desires and aspirations, with society's expectations often shaping an individual's pursuit of idealized beauty, success, and personal satisfaction. For Jocelyn Wildenstein, the quest for perfection would come at a considerable cost, both physically and emotionally.

Her journey to achieve a particular standard of beauty through cosmetic surgery would come to define her public persona, but the price she paid for this transformation was far greater than mere financial expenditure or the physical toll of numerous procedures. It was a sacrifice that would affect her relationships, her mental health, and her sense of self, ultimately leading to profound consequences in her life.

Jocelyn Wildenstein's transformation was not initially driven by the desire to conform to society's traditional standards of beauty. Instead, her quest for perfection was deeply personal. Motivated by a love of art, beauty, and the exotic animals she adored, particularly the grace of big cats, Jocelyn envisioned herself embodying these qualities.

Her surgeries, particularly the changes to her eyes, cheekbones, and jawline, were an attempt to create a more striking, wild, and unique appearance. The goal was not simply to alter her face for the sake of vanity, but to reshape herself into a form that resonated with her inner vision of beauty.

However, the desire for a flawless appearance is rarely devoid of complications. For Jocelyn, this pursuit was not just a personal journey of transformation but one that took place under the intense scrutiny of the media and public eye. The notion of beauty, often defined by youth, symmetry, and the natural grace of facial features, became an obsession for Jocelyn, yet it was also a double-edged sword.

As she moved further down the path of cosmetic surgery, the line between artistic self-expression and societal expectations blurred. Her decision to alter her appearance was not simply a reflection of her own desires, but was also influenced by external pressures, namely, the desire to maintain relevance, youth, and beauty in an unforgiving social environment.

The financial cost of Jocelyn's transformation was staggering. By some estimates, she spent millions of dollars over the course of several decades on cosmetic procedures, including facelifts, eye lifts, liposuction, rhinoplasty, and countless other surgeries.

The expense of these procedures was a testament to her commitment to her vision of beauty, but it also came with a significant personal cost. The heavy financial burden placed on Jocelyn, and, for a time, on her husband Alec Wildenstein, was a reflection of just how far she was willing to go in her pursuit of perfection.

The physical toll, however, was even more profound. The cumulative effects of multiple surgeries left Jocelyn with a face that had been altered so extensively that it began to look less like her original self and more like an entirely different person.

While Jocelyn herself may have viewed these changes as necessary steps toward achieving her idealized look, the physical consequences were apparent. The tightness of her skin, the unnatural shape of her cheekbones, and the exaggerated contour of her eyes were the result of repeated surgical procedures, and over time, the toll on her body became clear.

But the physical toll was not just cosmetic. Each surgery required recovery time, often leaving Jocelyn in pain and discomfort as her body adjusted to the changes. The psychological strain of such extensive procedures, coupled with the public's scrutiny, was an often-overlooked aspect of her journey. The process of seeking perfection through surgery is not a mere physical act; it is emotionally and psychologically consuming, leading to feelings of insecurity, fear, and anxiety.

The pursuit of perfection did not only affect Jocelyn's relationship with her own body, but also with those around her. One of the most notable aspects of her story was how her transformation impacted her marriage to Alec Wildenstein. When Jocelyn first met Alec, their relationship was one of passion and shared interests, particularly in the realm of art and beauty. Alec, who came from an art dealer and auctioneer background, had a deep appreciation for aesthetics, which matched Jocelyn's own desire to live a life surrounded by beauty.

However, as Jocelyn's surgeries became more frequent and extreme, it became increasingly difficult for Alec to understand or support her choices. The intimate bond they once shared began to strain under the weight of her transformation. There were reports that Alec, at times, expressed concern over her decisions, particularly when the results of her surgeries became more visibly extreme. The deterioration of their relationship would eventually culminate in their divorce, a separation that would not only be influenced by their personal issues but also by the growing gulf between Jocelyn's appearance and Alec's perception of her.

Jocelyn's pursuit of physical perfection also created a sense of alienation. She became increasingly isolated, with her self-image tied to the changes she made to her face and body. Her identity, once rooted in her marriage and her life as a socialite, began to revolve around her physical transformation.

As her surgeries continued, she became more distant from the people who once supported her. Her family, friends, and even the public started to see her less as a person and more as a living spectacle, a figure to be admired or mocked for her extreme appearance. The loneliness that came with this alienation, combined with the inner struggles of navigating the public's reaction to her changing face, weighed heavily on her emotional well-being.

One of the most poignant costs of Jocelyn's transformation was the constant media attention that followed her every move. While the tabloids initially focused on her wealth and lifestyle, once her surgeries became more dramatic, the media spotlight shifted almost exclusively to her appearance.

The public's fascination with her transformation often bordered on obsession, as photographers and journalists eagerly chronicled her evolving face. The "Catwoman" moniker, which had initially emerged as a sensational nickname, soon became synonymous with Jocelyn's identity, reducing her to a figure of mockery and spectacle.

In her case, the pursuit of beauty and perfection was no longer a private endeavor; it was a public one. Every new procedure was met with an avalanche of media coverage, and each new photo of Jocelyn in public prompted widespread commentary.

While many of these reactions were critical, even cruel, the media's relentless focus on her appearance meant that her life was no longer her own. She was trapped in a cycle where her self-image was constantly being reframed by the opinions of others. Her choice to pursue cosmetic surgery became inextricably linked to the way she was perceived by the world, often at the expense of her emotional well-being.

Perhaps the greatest price Jocelyn paid for her pursuit of perfection was the toll it took on her mental health. The decision to undergo multiple surgeries was not an easy one, and it came with its own set of emotional and psychological consequences. There was the ever-present fear of rejection, of not meeting the idealized standards of beauty she had set for herself. As she underwent more surgeries, there were growing feelings of insecurity and anxiety, as she wrestled with whether the results would meet her expectations.

The emotional strain of constantly altering her appearance is a reality often overlooked when discussing cosmetic surgery. For Jocelyn, the pursuit of perfection was not simply about improving her looks; it became an obsession. She sought to become something other than herself, pushing the boundaries of what was possible in a quest for an unattainable ideal.

The toll on her mental health was profound, as the very act of transforming her face became a way of distancing herself from her true self. The repeated surgeries and their results raised questions about her own sense of identity. Who was Jocelyn Wildenstein without the surgery, without the alterations?

Additionally, the public's harsh judgment further exacerbated her feelings of inadequacy. The media's constant criticism, the derisive comments, and the ridicule created a situation where she could not escape the psychological effects of her decision. Her self-worth became entwined with her physical appearance, leaving her vulnerable to the emotional consequences of living in a world that placed so much value on external beauty.

The pursuit of perfection came at a significant price for Jocelyn Wildenstein, a price that was measured not only in financial costs and physical alterations but in the emotional and psychological toll it took on her life. Her story is a poignant reminder of the dangers of equating self-worth with external beauty, and the sacrifices that can come with striving for an unattainable ideal.

While Jocelyn's transformation is often viewed with judgment and derision, it is also a reflection of the complex interplay between personal desires and societal pressures. In her search for perfection, Jocelyn paid a price that extended far beyond the scalpel, one that reshaped her life in ways she could not have anticipated, leaving her with a legacy that will forever be tied to her appearance.

8.1 Physical, Emotional, and Financial Costs of Transformation

Jocelyn Wildenstein's transformation through cosmetic surgery is a remarkable and often tragic example of the high costs associated with pursuing an idealized image of beauty. While the visible results of her many surgeries are a testament to the lengths she went to achieve her vision of perfection, the physical, emotional, and financial tolls are less immediately apparent but far more profound. Her journey into transformation was not merely about reshaping her face or body, it was a complex process that entailed deep sacrifices on multiple fronts.

The most obvious cost of Jocelyn Wildenstein's transformation is the physical toll on her body. Over the course of several decades, Jocelyn underwent numerous surgeries, some estimates suggest more than 100 procedures, many of them invasive, extreme, and performed with the goal of reshaping her facial features. This pursuit of a dramatic, almost animalistic look, especially with regard to her feline-inspired eyes and pronounced cheekbones, was physically demanding, not just in terms of the procedures themselves, but in their cumulative effects.

Each surgery, no matter how expertly performed, carried with it inherent risks: anesthesia complications, infections, scarring, and prolonged recovery times. Cosmetic surgeries often require the patient to go under general anesthesia, which comes with its own set of dangers, including the possibility of an allergic reaction or complications related to the cardiovascular system. Jocelyn's repeated surgeries meant that her body was continuously subjected to these risks, and the recovery process each time became increasingly difficult as her body aged.

The surgeries also left lasting, sometimes irreversible, marks on her face. The tightness in her skin, the unnatural angle of her eyes, the puffiness in her cheeks, each of these was the result of a procedure that altered her anatomy. As time passed, the repeated strain on her skin and underlying tissues caused them to lose elasticity, which made recovery more challenging. There were reports of Jocelyn experiencing discomfort as a result of the tightness in her skin, which, in turn, affected her daily life. Her extreme facial features, which were originally designed to enhance her beauty and uniqueness, instead left her with a face that looked increasingly artificial and unnatural.

Moreover, these physical changes became permanent. Unlike temporary cosmetic procedures like Botox or fillers, many of Jocelyn's surgeries involved more invasive changes to her bone structure, including her cheekbones and jawline. The permanence of these alterations meant that even if she had chosen to stop the surgeries, she could never fully reverse the changes. The physical toll of these alterations was not just about discomfort and scars,it was about the loss of her original identity, with each surgery leaving her looking less like her former self.

While the physical costs are visible, the emotional costs of Jocelyn's transformation are far more complex and harder to quantify. The decision to undergo surgery after surgery was deeply personal, but it was also deeply tied to her self-image and identity. Jocelyn, who had been raised with a love for beauty and art, viewed her transformation as a form of self-expression. She sought to embody the grace and elegance of the exotic animals she admired, particularly big cats, but over time, this transformation became a way to escape her own insecurities and attempt to control her narrative.

One of the most profound emotional costs came from Jocelyn's struggle with self-image. Cosmetic surgery, when approached with the desire to alter one's natural features, often reflects deeper feelings of dissatisfaction or the desire to live up to a certain ideal. Jocelyn's surgeries were not solely motivated by a wish to enhance her beauty; they were driven by an inner desire to reshape herself in a way that made her feel more powerful, more secure, and more in control of her life. But the more she altered her appearance, the more detached she became from her authentic self. She gradually began to lose sight of who she was beneath the surgeries, and this internal struggle affected her mental and emotional state.

There are moments when Jocelyn has discussed her surgeries with a sense of regret, particularly as the public's scrutiny grew harsher and the results of her surgeries became more pronounced. She spoke of feeling misunderstood and alone, especially as her appearance increasingly became a subject of ridicule and mockery. What began as a personal pursuit to enhance her beauty and artistic vision became a source of deep emotional conflict, as the gap between her vision of herself and the way others saw her widened.

Furthermore, the repeated media attention and the nickname "Catwoman" created an emotional toll that went beyond the physical. Jocelyn was relentlessly photographed, and each new image sparked criticism, judgment, and even ridicule. The intense media scrutiny, paired with her own insecurities, eroded her self-confidence, as she was no longer seen as a person, but as a spectacle.

Over time, this emotional strain weighed heavily on her mental health, leading her to experience feelings of isolation, loneliness, and anxiety. The pressure of living up to the beauty ideals she had set for herself, while being publicly judged for every new alteration, created a perfect storm of emotional distress.

The emotional cost of Jocelyn's transformation was not just about how she saw herself, it was also about how she was seen by others. The public's perception of her became inextricably linked to her appearance, reducing her identity to the sum of her surgeries. In this way, her personal journey was never truly hers to own; it was shaped, criticized, and judged by the world around her.

The financial costs of Jocelyn Wildenstein's transformation are staggering, with some reports estimating that she spent upwards of $4 million on cosmetic surgery throughout her lifetime. These expenses were not limited to surgeries alone but also included the various treatments, consultations, and recovery periods that accompanied each procedure.

At the height of her fame, she had the resources to fund this costly lifestyle, thanks to her marriage to Alec Wildenstein, a wealthy art heir. Alec, who came from a family with deep ties to the art world and had a significant fortune, seemed to support her at first, indulging her desire to reshape her appearance.

However, over time, the financial strain of such extensive procedures became apparent. The expenses related to Jocelyn's surgeries likely put a strain on her marriage, especially as her appearance became more extreme. Her fixation on perfection through cosmetic enhancement came at the expense of their relationship, and their eventual divorce was partially attributed to these growing tensions. The emotional costs of their fractured relationship were compounded by the financial costs of their lavish lifestyle, which Jocelyn continued to maintain even after the dissolution of her marriage.

Beyond her personal finances, Jocelyn's surgeries were a source of scrutiny in the media. Her spending habits, particularly on her looks, became a symbol of excessive wealth and vanity. As the public's fascination with her appearance grew, the financial costs of her transformations became part of the larger narrative that surrounded her. The media often emphasized her wealth, as though her money was the root cause of her decision to undergo such extreme procedures.

One of the most troubling aspects of Jocelyn Wildenstein's pursuit of perfection is the way in which the physical, emotional, and financial costs intertwined, creating a cycle that perpetuated itself. Her desire to change her appearance through surgery, driven by a need to control her self-image, led her to make increasingly drastic decisions that took a toll on her health, her relationships, and her finances. The more surgeries she underwent, the more her public identity became linked to her appearance, and the more she was driven to alter herself in an attempt to meet the expectations she had created for herself.

This cycle was self-reinforcing: each new surgery was meant to correct or enhance what she had already done, but with each new alteration came more public attention, greater media scrutiny, and deeper emotional distress. The physical toll was compounded by the growing emotional toll of dealing with constant public judgment. The financial costs also mounted as her surgeries continued and her marriage fell apart, leaving her to bear the full weight of her transformation.

Jocelyn Wildenstein's journey to perfection, while extreme, is not unique in its exploration of the costs associated with altering one's body in pursuit of beauty. The physical, emotional, and financial tolls she paid are an essential part of her story, showing the complexities of the human desire for beauty and perfection. Her transformation, while pursued with the intention of self-expression and artistic vision, ultimately resulted in a loss of self-identity, strained relationships, and a legacy tied to a physical appearance that never fully met her expectations.

In the end, Jocelyn's pursuit of perfection was an example of the high price that often comes with altering one's body to fit an idealized image. The costs, both tangible and intangible, have left a lasting impact on her life, serving as a cautionary tale of the sacrifices made in the pursuit of beauty. Despite her outward appearance of success and wealth, Jocelyn's transformation came at a cost that was far more than what any surgery could remedy.

8.2 Struggling with Public and Personal Identity

Jocelyn Wildenstein's life has been an intricate dance between self-expression, personal desires, and societal pressures. Her pursuit of an idealized version of beauty through extreme cosmetic surgery was not only about changing her appearance but also a manifestation of a deeper struggle with her identity, both public and personal.

As her transformation progressed, she found herself at the center of a complex and often painful tension between how she saw herself and how the world saw her. Her journey reveals the emotional, psychological, and social costs of reshaping one's identity in the pursuit of an unattainable ideal. The struggle with her public and personal identity became one of the defining elements of her life, and the consequences of this struggle echo far beyond the physical changes to her face.

At its core, Jocelyn Wildenstein's decision to undergo numerous surgeries was not merely about altering her appearance, it was deeply tied to her quest for self-expression. Jocelyn's love for art, beauty, and the exotic grace of big cats drove her to seek a way to embody those qualities in her own appearance. Her surgeries were not random; they were intentional changes designed to make her feel more powerful, more aligned with the creatures she admired, and ultimately, more connected to her own inner vision of beauty.

However, this search for self-expression was complicated by Jocelyn's deeper internal struggles. From the start, she was aware of the cultural significance of beauty and the role it plays in one's sense of worth and acceptance. Born into a more modest upbringing in Switzerland, Jocelyn was not immune to the pressures placed on women to meet certain beauty standards. Throughout her life, she internalized these ideals, which led her to view physical beauty as a key component of her identity.

But, as her surgeries continued, Jocelyn's appearance became more and more detached from her original self. The repeated changes, especially to her face, left her with a look that was increasingly at odds with the woman she had been. The pursuit of this external ideal clashed with her internal sense of self, leaving her with a fragmented sense of identity.

While she may have seen her surgeries as a form of self-empowerment, there were moments when she grappled with feelings of disconnection from the person she had once been. The self she was trying to create through these procedures was a version of herself that was forever elusive. Instead of finding peace and fulfillment in her transformed body, Jocelyn began to struggle with a deep emotional disconnect, as though she was no longer sure who she truly was beneath the layers of surgical changes. This dissonance between her physical appearance and her emotional reality added to the psychological toll of her journey.

Jocelyn's struggles with her personal identity were only exacerbated by the public's reaction to her transformation. As her appearance changed, so did the public's perception of her, turning her into an object of fascination, ridicule, and often, cruelty. The media's intense focus on her surgeries reduced Jocelyn to a spectacle, an embodiment of beauty gone awry in the eyes of many. The nickname "Catwoman," which the press assigned to her, was an ironic commentary on her appearance and only solidified her status as an outsider in the world of high society.

The nickname itself speaks to the complexity of Jocelyn's relationship with her public identity. Initially, Jocelyn may have felt empowered by her transformation, as though she were becoming the very creature she admired. But as the media latched onto her appearance, it was as if her identity was hijacked, reduced to a superficial and almost cartoonish version of what she had tried to create. The more she altered her face, the more she became known not by her name, but by the nickname that emphasized her perceived monstrousness. This transformation from socialite to "Catwoman" was not one of empowerment—it was one of alienation.

As her surgeries became more extreme and the media's coverage of her intensified, Jocelyn found herself constantly scrutinized, and her identity became more and more dictated by public opinion. No longer seen as an individual with a unique story or accomplishments, she was instead objectified and her worth was measured by her physical transformation. This stripping away of her personal identity and the public's obsession with her appearance undoubtedly weighed heavily on her sense of self-worth. She became trapped in a feedback loop: the more she tried to align herself with her artistic and aesthetic vision, the more she became a symbol of excess, vanity, and derision in the eyes of the public.

The public's constant judgment contributed to Jocelyn's growing feelings of isolation. The media didn't just critique her appearance; it critiqued her character, her choices, and even her worth as a person. The pervasive nature of this criticism often led her to internalize those judgments, deepening her emotional distress. At times, it seemed as if the more she tried to assert control over her identity, the more the public seized that control, molding her into an icon of excess and obsession rather than a woman with agency over her own life.

Living in the public eye is a double-edged sword, especially when one's physical appearance becomes the central focus of public discourse. For Jocelyn, the emotional strain of being constantly scrutinized was immense. Her face, once a reflection of her personal desires, became the focal point of media attention. Her face was no longer just hers, it was a public commodity, something to be dissected, judged, and mocked.

The psychological effects of this constant attention were profound. Jocelyn was unable to escape the critical gaze of the media, and the more she tried to live her life, the more her identity became bound up in how others viewed her. For someone already struggling with feelings of insecurity and self-doubt, the relentless media attention compounded these emotions. Her identity, which had once been tied to her personal relationships, her wealth, and her love of art and beauty, was now inseparable from her public image. The "Catwoman" moniker came to define her in the public's eyes, rendering her invisible as an individual beyond her physical appearance.

In many ways, the media turned her transformation into a tragedy, a cautionary tale of what can happen when one becomes consumed by the pursuit of beauty and perfection. But for Jocelyn, the emotional toll of living as a caricature in the eyes of the world was much more than a public spectacle; it was a deeply personal tragedy. Her self-worth, which she had once tied to her beauty and her physical appearance, was now constantly challenged and ridiculed. The emotional toll of this constant judgment and alienation contributed to a growing sense of loneliness and isolation.

One of the most significant aspects of Jocelyn's struggle with her public and personal identity was the tension between authenticity and societal acceptance. As she altered her body, Jocelyn sought to create an image that she felt would make her more powerful and attractive, a reflection of her inner desires and vision. However, this desire for acceptance often conflicted with her pursuit of authenticity. What began as a personal journey to align her exterior with her inner sense of beauty eventually became a battle to retain a sense of self in a world that refused to see her beyond her physical changes.

The desire for external validation and the need to be seen as beautiful according to society's standards led Jocelyn to prioritize her appearance over her true self. Despite her attempts to express her unique vision, she was reduced to a public figure whose worth was measured by how closely her appearance matched the idealized notions of beauty that society often imposes on women. Jocelyn's public identity became a commodity, something to be consumed, critiqued, and dissected, with little regard for the person behind the transformations.

Her struggle for authenticity was not merely a fight for self-expression, it was a battle for recognition as a whole person, beyond the surgeries and the headlines. In many ways, her public identity became a mask, one that she herself may have struggled to reconcile with her true self. As her appearance grew more extreme, her emotional dissonance grew, leaving her trapped in a cycle of attempting to fulfill an ideal that was never fully attainable, even in her own eyes.

Jocelyn Wildenstein's life story is an exploration of the intricate relationship between public and personal identity, and the emotional and psychological costs that can result from living in the spotlight. Her physical transformation, while initially an attempt to express her artistic vision and personal desires, became a battleground for her sense of self. The media's fixation on her appearance and the relentless judgment she faced created an overwhelming sense of alienation, leaving her struggling with who she was beneath the surface.

The price of reshaping her identity, both physically and emotionally, was far steeper than she may have anticipated. Her public identity, shaped by the media and the public's expectations, never fully aligned with her inner sense of self. In the end, Jocelyn's struggle with public and personal identity serves as a powerful reminder of the dangers of allowing external perceptions to define one's worth. Her story highlights the difficulty of balancing the desire for self-expression with the pressures of societal expectations, and the profound toll

it can take on one's emotional and psychological
well-being.

CHAPTER NINE: A MARRIAGE UNRAVELS

The story of Jocelyn Wildenstein's marriage to Alec Wildenstein is as much about the disintegration of a personal relationship as it is about the collapse of a carefully constructed image of wealth, power, and beauty. Their union, once seen as a fairytale romance between a beautiful young woman and a wealthy art heir, became strained by the emotional, financial, and personal tensions that arose over the years. The unraveling of their marriage is a poignant chapter in Jocelyn's life, one that reflects the complexities of love, identity, and the cost of living in the public eye.

When Jocelyn Wildenstein first met Alec Wildenstein, her life seemed to take a turn toward the extraordinary. Alec, a wealthy heir to the Wildenstein art dynasty, came from a family renowned for its involvement in the world of art, with interests spanning galleries, auctions, and the high society of New York and Paris.

Jocelyn, a Swiss beauty with aspirations of grandeur, quickly integrated herself into this world of luxury and excess. She was captivated not only by Alec's wealth but by the opportunities his family's legacy offered her. Their courtship and eventual marriage were marked by a whirlwind of glamour, lavish parties, luxurious homes, and a life few could dream of.

Alec was captivated by Jocelyn's beauty, while she was drawn to his powerful position in the art world. For Jocelyn, this marriage seemed to be the perfect way to attain the life she had always dreamed of, one that matched the beauty and sophistication she admired in the high-society world she was now part of. However, the union was not simply based on love. It was also rooted in a mutual understanding of status, wealth, and the expectations that came with both.

Their marriage, which began with an almost fairytale-like quality, was defined by excess, luxury homes, expensive cars, private jets, and international travel. The couple was regularly seen in the most exclusive venues, rubbing elbows with the rich and famous. Jocelyn, a woman of ambition and self-expression, found herself constantly in the limelight, both as Alec's wife and as a symbol of beauty and wealth. The marriage allowed her to indulge in her passion for art, fashion, and beauty, and she often accompanied Alec to auctions, art exhibitions, and galas.

However, the perfection of their life together was superficial, and beneath the surface, cracks were beginning to form. While they appeared to be a picture-perfect couple from the outside, their personal lives became increasingly complicated over time.

As the years went by, the relationship between Jocelyn and Alec became strained. Despite the lavish lifestyle and public appearances, the couple struggled privately with emotional disconnect and growing resentment. Alec, who had a reputation for being cold and distant, became increasingly preoccupied with his business interests, particularly his family's art dealings.

His wealth and legacy, which had initially seemed like a shared foundation for their marriage, began to serve as a source of tension between the two. Jocelyn, who had married Alec partly for his status and wealth, was beginning to feel emotionally neglected as he turned his attention elsewhere.

On her side, Jocelyn's emotional needs were not being met in the way she had hoped. The more she invested in her appearance, the more she altered her identity through cosmetic surgery, the more disconnected she became from the person her husband had originally married. While Alec continued to spend time in the world of art, philanthropy, and high-society dealings, Jocelyn's obsession with her appearance and her transformation grew.

The gap between them widened. Jocelyn felt that her beauty, once the cornerstone of her identity, was no longer enough to keep her husband's attention. The pressures of maintaining their lavish lifestyle also took their toll on the marriage. With wealth came a constant desire for more, and the need to maintain a façade of perfection, whether it was through their outwardly perfect home or Jocelyn's ever-evolving image, became more demanding.

Alec, who was not particularly emotionally expressive, became increasingly distant as Jocelyn's focus shifted toward her physical transformation. While she poured herself into her appearance, he withdrew into his business and private interests. The emotional neglect, coupled with the constant societal pressures they both faced, made the relationship feel increasingly hollow. The glamour and opulence of their life could no longer mask the growing dissatisfaction within their marriage.

One of the most public and painful blows to the marriage came when Alec was found to be involved in an extramarital affair. This was a turning point that marked the unraveling of their relationship. For Jocelyn, this revelation was a devastating betrayal. While their marriage had been characterized by mutual reliance on each other's status and wealth, the affair shattered the illusion of their perfect life. Alec's infidelity not only revealed the emotional rift between the couple but also exposed the fractures in their shared vision of their marriage.

In the aftermath of the affair, Jocelyn was left to deal with the emotional fallout. For someone whose sense of self-worth was closely tied to her beauty and her relationship with Alec, the infidelity was a blow that struck at her core. Her self-esteem, already fragile due to the changes she had made to her own body, suffered further damage. The affair also highlighted the growing disconnect between them, the emotional distance that had formed over the years had now manifested in a way that could no longer be ignored.

Despite the affair, Jocelyn chose to stay in the marriage for a time, hoping to repair the damage and rebuild the trust that had been lost. She continued to invest in her image, perhaps as a way to regain her confidence and assert her power in a relationship that was rapidly deteriorating. However, the damage was done, and the emotional strain of trying to repair something that seemed irreparable began to take its toll.

The final blow to Jocelyn and Alec's marriage came when they filed for divorce in 1999. The breakdown of their marriage was not just a personal tragedy but a financial one as well. With their separation came a high-profile legal battle over money and assets, with Jocelyn fighting for a substantial portion of the Wildenstein family fortune.

The divorce settlement, which was reportedly worth hundreds of millions of dollars, highlighted the financial aspect of their relationship, the role that wealth and status had played in holding them together, even when the emotional connection had long since faded.

Jocelyn's battle for her share of Alec's fortune became a symbol of the complex dynamics of their marriage. While Alec had spent years amassing a vast fortune, Jocelyn had invested much of her life into maintaining a particular image, an image that relied heavily on the wealth and status Alec had provided.

When their marriage crumbled, Jocelyn found herself not only grieving the emotional loss but also fighting for the financial security that had been part of their union. The financial battle that followed the divorce was as contentious as the emotional one, revealing how intertwined their lives had become with money and public perception.

For Jocelyn, the divorce was not just the end of a marriage but also the loss of the lavish life she had become accustomed to. While she received a large settlement, the emotional toll of the divorce left scars that would linger for years to come. It also marked the end of an era, an era in which she had been defined by her marriage to Alec and the high-society lifestyle that came with it. The dissolution of their marriage represented the collapse of an illusion, one in which beauty, wealth, and status could not prevent the unraveling of their personal lives.

After the divorce, Jocelyn found herself struggling to redefine her identity in the aftermath of the marriage. She was no longer Alec Wildenstein's wife, no longer a symbol of a glamorous, high-society marriage. The world that had once been hers was now inaccessible, and she was left to navigate a new life that was free from the trappings of wealth and the constant media attention. For a woman who had defined herself by her beauty and her marriage, this was a difficult transition.

Her physical transformation, once a form of self-expression and empowerment, now seemed to represent a woman trying to hold onto a version of herself that was fading away. The emotional scars from the breakdown of her marriage would continue to affect her, and she was left to contend with the legacy of a relationship that had both shaped and shattered her sense of self.

The unraveling of Jocelyn and Alec Wildenstein's marriage is a stark reminder of the complexities that lie behind the polished façade of wealth, beauty, and high society. While their union began as a glamorous and seemingly perfect match, it ultimately unraveled due to emotional neglect, infidelity, and the increasing tensions between personal desires and external expectations. The breakdown of their marriage not only marked the end of a chapter in Jocelyn's life but also set the stage for the next phase of her identity struggle.

As the public watched their high-profile divorce and the accompanying legal battles, it became clear that the price of their glamorous life was far higher than either of them had anticipated. For Jocelyn, the end of her marriage was a painful reminder of the emotional costs of living in a world where beauty, wealth, and power often come at the expense of personal connection and authenticity.

9.1 Infidelity and Betrayal

In the tumultuous narrative of Jocelyn Wildenstein's marriage to Alec Wildenstein, the themes of infidelity and betrayal were pivotal in marking the turning point in their relationship. What began as a glamorous fairytale romance eventually crumbled under the weight of emotional distance, unmet expectations, and the eventual discovery of infidelity.

The impact of Alec's extramarital affair on their marriage was far-reaching, creating ripples that not only affected their personal lives but also their public personas and legacy. The complex dynamics of betrayal, trust, and emotional pain serve as a lens through which to examine the disintegration of a marriage that had once been defined by luxury, beauty, and social status.

In the early years of their marriage, Jocelyn and Alec Wildenstein seemed like the quintessential power couple. They had everything that many people aspire to: immense wealth, high-society status, and a seemingly perfect relationship. Alec, an heir to the Wildenstein art dynasty, had access to the finest things in life, luxury homes, private jets, art collections, and the kind of social prominence that few could rival. Jocelyn, with her beauty and elegance, became the perfect complement to his lifestyle, fitting into the world of elite New York and European circles with grace.

For Jocelyn, this marriage represented the fulfillment of her lifelong dreams. She had always envisioned herself as part of the glamorous world of high society, and Alec seemed like the ticket to that life. As their relationship deepened, Jocelyn's sense of self became increasingly tied to the wealth and prestige that Alec's family provided. She poured herself into the role of a glamorous wife, attending exclusive events, traveling the world, and living a life that many could only dream of. However, beneath the surface of this seemingly perfect existence, cracks were beginning to form.

Alec, a man of few emotional expressions, became more absorbed in his family's art dealings and business interests. His emotional detachment from Jocelyn, coupled with her growing obsession with beauty and her physical transformation, created a widening chasm between them. The illusion of marital harmony was slowly eroded as both partners retreated into their own worlds, neglecting the intimacy and connection that should have defined their relationship.

The turning point in their marriage came when Jocelyn discovered that Alec had been having an affair. For Jocelyn, who had already been feeling neglected and emotionally distant from her husband, this revelation was a devastating betrayal. The woman who had once been the center of Alec's life, the young, beautiful wife he had married, was now faced with the painful reality that her husband's affections were elsewhere. Alec's affair was not just an act of infidelity; it was an emotional rupture that exposed the deep-seated problems in their relationship.

For Jocelyn, the affair represented the ultimate betrayal. Throughout their marriage, she had placed a great deal of her self-worth in the relationship, believing that Alec's love and devotion were a reflection of her own beauty and worth. When Alec's infidelity came to light, it shattered the very foundation of her identity. The betrayal went beyond the physical act of cheating; it was a rejection of the person she had believed herself to be within the context of their marriage. It made her question whether she was truly enough for him, or if, after all the surgeries and transformations, she was still the woman he had fallen in love with.

The emotional devastation Jocelyn felt after learning of the affair was compounded by the public nature of their lives. As a prominent couple in New York and beyond, their marriage was under constant scrutiny, and the discovery of Alec's infidelity became a high-profile scandal. It was not just a private matter, it was something that the world would see, judge, and gossip about. Jocelyn's sense of humiliation was profound, as the woman who had carefully crafted an image of wealth and beauty now had to face the fact that her marriage, and her sense of self, were unraveling in front of the public eye.

The emotional fallout of Alec's affair was far-reaching, and the damage was not limited to the breakdown of their relationship. For Jocelyn, this betrayal forced her to confront her own insecurities, particularly concerning her physical appearance and her role in their marriage. As a woman whose sense of self was deeply entwined with her beauty, the idea that her husband had sought out another woman was a blow to her already fragile self-esteem. The affair challenged the very foundation of her identity, what had once been the centerpiece of their marriage, her beauty, now seemed insufficient to keep Alec faithful.

In the aftermath of the affair, Jocelyn was forced to grapple with a painful sense of rejection. Despite her efforts to transform herself physically through numerous cosmetic procedures, she was no longer able to hold onto the image of the perfect wife. Alec's affair symbolized a failure of the relationship that Jocelyn had invested so much in, emotionally, financially, and physically. She had sacrificed much of her true self in pursuit of an ideal of beauty that she believed would keep her husband's attention, but in the end, this transformation was not enough to sustain their marriage.

Trust, once broken, is exceedingly difficult to rebuild. For Jocelyn, the breach in trust was profound, and the emotional toll was devastating. The affair undermined the security she had felt in the relationship and led to feelings of betrayal that ran deeper than just infidelity. It created a space between her and Alec that was not easily bridged. No amount of wealth, status, or physical beauty could heal the wounds caused by emotional neglect and unfaithfulness.

The public nature of their marriage only heightened the sense of betrayal and humiliation Jocelyn experienced. As a prominent socialite and the wife of an influential businessman, Jocelyn's life was always under the public eye. The media, eager to report on the personal lives of celebrities and the wealthy elite, quickly latched onto the scandal surrounding Alec's affair. The affair became a topic of public discourse, with tabloids and gossip columns offering constant commentary on the state of their marriage.

This exposure turned the private pain of Jocelyn's betrayal into a public spectacle. Her once-polished image as the beautiful, affluent wife of Alec Wildenstein was tarnished. She became the subject of mockery and gossip, with many questioning her worth and speculating about her role in the dissolution of the marriage. The media's portrayal of her as a victim of Alec's infidelity added another layer of complexity to her emotional distress. As the press relentlessly focused on her changing appearance and the high-profile nature of her divorce, Jocelyn found herself at the center of a narrative she could not control.

For a woman whose sense of identity had been built in part on the glamour and luxury of her marriage, this public exposure was another form of betrayal. The world saw her as an object of fascination, rather than as a woman grappling with the pain of betrayal and the collapse of her marriage. The media's portrayal of her as a "cat-faced" symbol of excess further deepened her sense of disconnection from her true self. She was not just a woman who had been hurt by her husband's infidelity, she was reduced to a caricature, a figure of ridicule in the eyes of the public.

The infidelity in her marriage and the subsequent fallout played a significant role in the evolution of Jocelyn Wildenstein's physical transformation. In many ways, her decision to undergo extreme cosmetic surgery was intertwined with her emotional and psychological state during this period.

As her marriage deteriorated and her sense of self was shattered by Alec's betrayal, Jocelyn may have sought solace in the idea of recreating herself. The physical changes she made to her face and body, her surgeries and transformations, became a way to cope with the emotional pain of her marital breakdown.

However, these transformations also reflected a deep internal struggle. While she may have believed that altering her appearance would make her feel more powerful or in control, it only further isolated her from her true self. As her relationship with Alec crumbled, so too did her ability to recognize herself in the mirror.

The changes she made to her body were, in many ways, an attempt to protect herself from the pain of rejection and betrayal. Yet, the more she transformed, the more disconnected she became from the woman she had once been. This cycle of physical alteration, driven by emotional pain, became a way to hide from the trauma of her marriage's collapse.

Alec Wildenstein's infidelity was a defining moment in Jocelyn Wildenstein's life. It was not just a betrayal of the marriage but a violation of the trust and emotional investment she had made over the years. The impact of the affair reverberated through her personal life, her sense of self-worth, and her public image. For Jocelyn, the emotional fallout of the betrayal was profound, and the scars left by Alec's unfaithfulness would continue to affect her long after their divorce.

The unraveling of their marriage, marked by infidelity and betrayal, highlights the fragility of relationships built on external factors like wealth, beauty, and status. While Jocelyn had initially defined herself by her marriage to Alec and her place in the world of high society, the affair forced her to confront a painful truth: these external markers of identity could not shield her from the emotional turmoil of a broken relationship. In the end, Alec's infidelity was not just a betrayal of their marriage, it was a turning point that irrevocably altered Jocelyn's understanding of herself and her place in the world.

9.2 The Explosive Divorce Trial

The divorce between Jocelyn Wildenstein and Alec Wildenstein was not just a personal tragedy, but also a highly publicized spectacle that captivated the media and the public. The legal battle, which lasted for years, was filled with drama, financial disputes, and intense media scrutiny, becoming one of the most explosive divorce trials of its time.

The trial was not just a legal process; it became a battle for identity, wealth, and power, with both sides fighting fiercely for what they believed they were entitled to. The media's involvement only heightened the intensity, as Jocelyn and Alec's bitter divorce became a high-stakes game of public perception, with both individuals seeking to control their narrative.

By the time Jocelyn and Alec Wildenstein's divorce trial began, their marriage had already been through significant turmoil. The infidelity and emotional estrangement that had characterized their relationship for years had finally taken its toll. The public discovery of Alec's affair had been the breaking point, but the cracks in the marriage were apparent long before the scandal hit the media. Jocelyn, who had dedicated much of her life to her marriage and her image as Alec's wife, was left in the wake of a relationship that no longer offered the emotional connection she had once hoped for.

The divorce came in 1999, after years of emotional neglect, public humiliation, and growing tension between the two. The Wildenstein family's vast fortune, estimated to be in the billions, added a complicated financial dimension to the divorce. Jocelyn, who had become accustomed to a lifestyle of luxury and excess, was determined to secure her future and maintain the opulence to which she had grown accustomed. Alec, on the other hand, was not only fighting for his wealth but also for control over his reputation and the legacy of his family's name.

The stakes of the divorce were incredibly high. Both parties had something to lose, but it was Jocelyn who stood to lose the most in terms of public image. While Alec was already entrenched in the world of art and high society, Jocelyn's identity had been inseparable from her role as his wife. This public divorce, fueled by bitterness and resentment, would impact their reputations for years to come.

The legal proceedings in the Wildenstein divorce were as dramatic as the marriage itself. Jocelyn, determined to secure a financial settlement worthy of the extravagant lifestyle she had become accustomed to, fought for a substantial portion of Alec's wealth. The Wildenstein family fortune, built on a legacy of art dealing and investments, was one of the largest and most influential in the world. As part of the divorce, Jocelyn was entitled to a share of this wealth, but the exact amount was contested.

At the heart of the legal battle was Jocelyn's request for a massive divorce settlement, reportedly valued at $2.5 billion. This sum was based on her claim that she had given up her career and personal interests to support Alec's business ventures and lifestyle. The magnitude of this demand shocked many observers and set the stage for a prolonged and contentious legal fight. Alec, who was unwilling to part with such a large portion of his fortune, fought back, insisting that Jocelyn had already received ample financial support over the years and that her request was unreasonable.

The legal teams for both sides were fierce, with the lawyers working tirelessly to build cases that would prove their client's entitlement to the fortune. For Jocelyn, this divorce was not just about money; it was also about ensuring that she could continue to live the luxurious life she had grown accustomed to. For Alec, the divorce trial was an opportunity to preserve his family's wealth and reputation, as well as to regain control over a situation that had spiraled out of his control.

One of the most heated aspects of the divorce trial was the argument over the family's assets. Jocelyn's team argued that her contributions to the marriage, both emotional and financial, deserved recognition and compensation. They also sought to highlight the ways in which Alec's infidelity and neglect had affected her. Alec's legal team, meanwhile, focused on challenging the legitimacy of Jocelyn's demands and minimizing her share of the fortune.

In addition to the financial aspects, the trial also delved
into the personal dynamics of the marriage, with both
sides attempting to paint a picture of the other as either
emotionally abusive or neglectful. Alec's infidelity and
emotional coldness were central points of contention,
while Jocelyn's physical transformation through
cosmetic surgery became a topic of public fascination.

What made the Wildenstein divorce trial even more
explosive was the extensive media coverage it received.
The Wildenstein name, synonymous with wealth, art,
and high society, was already a subject of public
fascination. The divorce added a new layer of intrigue,
as reporters and tabloids raced to cover every detail of
the proceedings. Jocelyn's transformation, which had
already garnered significant attention, became an even
larger focal point during the trial.

The media was not just reporting on the facts; they were
creating a narrative. Jocelyn's appearance, which had
changed dramatically due to cosmetic surgeries, was
often a point of ridicule and fascination. The tabloids

gleefully referred to her as the "Catwoman" and speculated about the psychological reasons behind her drastic transformations. This media frenzy, which often sensationalized her appearance, took the focus away from the substantive issues of the trial and turned her into a caricature.

While Jocelyn was depicted as a woman seeking a massive financial windfall, Alec was portrayed as a distant, aloof figure who had been unfaithful to his wife. The public nature of the trial meant that their personal struggles, infidelity, financial disputes, and emotional alienation—were laid bare for the world to see. This intense public scrutiny only added to the emotional toll that the divorce took on both Jocelyn and Alec.

The media's portrayal of the couple also affected the way they were perceived in society. Jocelyn, whose public image had always been tightly managed, was now seen through the lens of her divorce trial. The tabloids painted her as a woman who had used her beauty to manipulate her husband and secure her lavish lifestyle, but who was now seen as a victim of his betrayal. Alec, on the other hand, was painted as a wealthy businessman who had failed to live up to his responsibilities as a husband and had sought solace in the arms of another woman.

The media's constant coverage of the trial made it impossible for either of them to escape the public eye. Their private pain became a public spectacle, and the divorce trial was not just a legal process but a form of entertainment for many people.

After years of legal battles, the Wildenstein divorce was finally settled in 1999. Jocelyn received a reported $2.5 billion as part of the settlement, making it one of the largest divorce settlements in history at the time. The financial settlement, while substantial, did little to heal the emotional wounds inflicted by the breakdown of the marriage. Despite the money, Jocelyn found herself at the center of a public narrative that would continue to follow her for years to come.

The settlement was a reflection of the complexities of
the case. While Jocelyn had been awarded a large sum, it
was clear that both parties had lost something significant
in the process. For Alec, the financial settlement meant
parting with a large portion of his family's wealth, but it
also allowed him to move on from the public humiliation
of the trial. For Jocelyn, the settlement provided the
financial security she had fought for, but it also
underscored the fact that her marriage, and the life she
had built around it, had come to an end.

In the aftermath of the trial, both Jocelyn and Alec faced
the challenge of rebuilding their lives and reputations.
For Jocelyn, the financial windfall allowed her to
maintain a life of luxury, but it did little to erase the
emotional scars left by the divorce. The media continued
to follow her, scrutinizing her every move, and she was
left to navigate a new identity outside of her marriage to
Alec.

The Wildenstein divorce trial was a defining moment in
the lives of both Jocelyn and Alec. It marked the end of a

marriage that had been built on wealth, power, and societal expectations, but it also left both parties grappling with the long-term consequences of their public and personal actions. The trial was not just about the division of assets; it was about identity, control, and the price of fame.

For Jocelyn, the divorce trial was a painful reminder of the fragility of her identity, which had been intertwined with her marriage to Alec. The public nature of the trial, coupled with the media frenzy surrounding her appearance and her financial demands, meant that her personal pain was laid bare for the world to see. Alec, too, faced public backlash, and his reputation as a powerful art dealer was marred by the scandal of his infidelity and the bitter legal battle.

The Wildenstein divorce trial became a symbol of the complexities of high-society relationships, wealth, and public perception. It was a spectacle that showcased not only the financial stakes of a high-profile divorce but also the emotional and psychological toll of living in the public eye. For both Jocelyn and Alec, the trial was a defining moment that left lasting scars on their personal lives and legacies.

CHAPTER TEN: THE BILLION-DOLLAR DIVORCE

The divorce between Jocelyn Wildenstein and Alec Wildenstein is often referred to as one of the most expensive and high-profile divorces in history, a legal battle that captured the world's attention. The financial stakes were astronomical, with Jocelyn's settlement reportedly amounting to a staggering $2.5 billion, a sum that would make it one of the largest divorce settlements ever recorded at the time.

The case became synonymous with excessive wealth, extravagant lifestyles, and the complexities of dividing assets when money, influence, and a family legacy are involved. The billion-dollar divorce was not merely a legal proceeding, it was a spectacle of excess, power, and emotional turmoil, a drama played out in the public eye that would shape both Jocelyn and Alec Wildenstein's futures for years to come.

Before the divorce trial, the marriage between Jocelyn and Alec Wildenstein had been a fairytale of wealth, glamour, and luxury. Alec, an heir to the Wildenstein family fortune, had built his empire on art dealings, investments, and an unparalleled network of powerful connections in the art world.

Jocelyn, a Swiss socialite with dreams of becoming part of the global elite, had found her place as Alec's glamorous wife. Together, they represented the height of opulence, living in lavish residences in New York, Paris, and other international hotspots, surrounded by priceless art, yachts, and the finest luxuries money could buy.

But beneath the surface, the marriage was strained. Jocelyn had sacrificed much of her personal ambitions and professional interests to support Alec's business ventures and to maintain the façade of a perfect marriage. Over time, as their relationship grew distant, the cracks in the relationship widened. Infidelity, emotional neglect, and a growing sense of dissatisfaction pushed Jocelyn to a breaking point. The affair Alec had with another woman, coupled with his increasing emotional distance, shattered the image of marital bliss that had once defined their relationship.

The decision to divorce was a long time coming. Jocelyn's emotional struggles and Alec's betrayal had built up over the years, and when the divorce finally became inevitable, it set the stage for an explosive legal battle. The divorce would not just be about emotional healing or the dissolution of a marriage; it would become a struggle for control over a vast fortune, legacy, and public image.

When the divorce proceedings began in 1999, it was clear that the financial stakes were going to be enormous. Jocelyn, who had been accustomed to a lifestyle of unimaginable wealth, sought a settlement that would allow her to continue living in the luxury she had become used to.

She argued that, over the years, she had contributed to the success of Alec's art empire and had sacrificed her own career ambitions and personal desires to support him and his business. She believed that she was entitled to a large portion of the Wildenstein family fortune, which was rumored to be worth billions.

Jocelyn's lawyers initially demanded a sum of $2.5 billion, which would not only cover her future living expenses but also compensate her for the sacrifices she had made throughout the marriage. This demand, however, was met with intense resistance from Alec and his legal team. Alec, fiercely protective of his family's wealth and legacy, argued that Jocelyn had already been well taken care of and that her demands were excessive.

The Wildenstein estate, which included valuable real estate properties, a collection of priceless artwork, horses, yachts, and other luxury items, became the central battleground in the divorce. Jocelyn sought to secure her share of these assets, demanding a significant portion of Alec's fortune, while Alec insisted that he had already provided ample financial support during their marriage. The legal teams for both sides went head-to-head in an all-out war, using every legal tactic at their disposal to achieve the best possible outcome for their clients.

One of the key points of contention was Jocelyn's desire for a substantial cash settlement that would allow her to maintain her lavish lifestyle. Alec's legal team argued that her demands were unreasonable and based on a skewed understanding of their marriage. Alec himself, however, remained largely silent throughout much of the legal proceedings, leaving the task of defending his interests to his legal representatives. His lack of emotional involvement in the case only fueled Jocelyn's sense of betrayal and resentment, making the divorce more acrimonious than it perhaps needed to be.

As the case continued, the media eagerly followed every development, adding a layer of public pressure to the proceedings. The sensational nature of the divorce, combined with the astronomical financial stakes, turned the trial into a public spectacle, with both sides' attorneys attempting to paint their clients in the best possible light. The image of Jocelyn, who had undergone numerous cosmetic surgeries to maintain her youthful appearance, was scrutinized by the press, while Alec's infidelity was laid bare for the world to see.

The divorce trial was as much about managing public perception as it was about settling financial matters. The media's coverage of the trial was relentless, focusing not only on the high-stakes financial negotiations but also on the personal lives of Jocelyn and Alec. Jocelyn, already a subject of media fascination due to her striking appearance and the rumors surrounding her surgeries, became the target of widespread criticism and ridicule. The tabloids gleefully referred to her as "Catwoman," mocking her physical transformation, while also portraying her as a calculating socialite who was seeking to extort Alec for every penny he had.

On the other hand, Alec was presented as a wealthy businessman and art dealer who had been deceived by his wife's obsession with her looks and her constant demands for more wealth. The media painted him as a figure of restraint and control, even as the story of his extramarital affair and neglect of Jocelyn's emotional needs came to light. The tabloids, eager for sensational stories, focused on the more salacious aspects of the case, with less attention paid to the complex emotional and financial negotiations happening behind closed doors.

For Jocelyn, the media frenzy was particularly damaging. Not only was her appearance the subject of constant scrutiny, but her character and motives were also questioned. The public perception of her, shaped largely by the media's portrayal, was one of a woman who had used her beauty and her marriage to Alec to gain access to unimaginable wealth and luxury. This image of Jocelyn as a manipulative gold-digger overshadowed the more nuanced reality of her emotional suffering and her desire for financial security.

Jocelyn's public image as the "Catwoman" also became a central narrative in the divorce trial. As her physical appearance became a focal point of the media's coverage, it was clear that her transformation had taken on a life of its own. The more she attempted to reshape her external appearance, the more the media scrutinized her, turning her into a public figure whose very identity seemed to be in question. The trial, in many ways, became a reflection of her struggle with identity, both personal and public.

After years of legal battles, the divorce was finally settled in 1999. Jocelyn was awarded a reported $2.5 billion in a financial settlement, a sum that made it one of the largest divorce settlements in history. The settlement included not only cash but also a portion of Alec's vast assets, including real estate holdings and art collections. It was a significant victory for Jocelyn, who had fought fiercely to maintain her lifestyle and secure her future.

The sum, however, came at a personal cost. While Jocelyn had achieved a financial victory, the public nature of the divorce left a lasting impact on her reputation. The media's portrayal of her as a woman obsessed with beauty and wealth overshadowed her claims of emotional and personal sacrifice. For Alec, the settlement was a necessary concession to end the legal battle, but it was also a painful loss of a significant portion of his fortune. The Wildenstein family's name, once associated with art and wealth, was now tainted by the public scandal surrounding the divorce.

In the aftermath of the divorce, both Jocelyn and Alec faced the challenge of rebuilding their lives and reputations. Jocelyn, despite her financial windfall, remained a subject of media fascination and often ridicule. She continued to live in the luxury she had become accustomed to, but her public image had been irreparably damaged. Alec, too, faced the consequences of the divorce, as his reputation as a wealthy art dealer was forever linked to the public scandal and his personal failings in the marriage.

The Wildenstein divorce was more than just a financial transaction; it was a turning point in both Jocelyn and Alec's lives. For Jocelyn, the billion-dollar settlement ensured that she would never have to worry about money again, but it also cemented her status as a figure of public fascination and, often, ridicule. She continued to live a life of luxury, but the price of that lifestyle was a public persona that was defined by scandal, surgery, and a seemingly endless quest for approval.

For Alec, the divorce marked the end of his marriage and the loss of a significant portion of his family's fortune. The emotional toll of the trial, combined with the public scrutiny of his affair and the subsequent media frenzy, forever altered his relationship with both his family and the public.

The billion-dollar divorce of Jocelyn and Alec Wildenstein was a spectacle that highlighted the complexities of wealth, marriage, and identity. The staggering financial settlement, the media circus, and the emotional fallout from the trial shaped both of their futures in ways that would reverberate for years to come. In the end, the divorce was a painful reminder of the price of perfection, both financially and emotionally, in a world where wealth, image, and public perception often collide.

10.1 Jocelyn's Record-Breaking Settlement

Jocelyn Wildenstein's divorce settlement with Alec Wildenstein is often cited as one of the largest in history, an outcome that was both a financial victory and a media spectacle. The settlement, reportedly worth $2.5 billion, placed Jocelyn at the center of one of the most high-profile and contentious divorce battles of the late 20th century.

Beyond the sheer size of the amount, the settlement encapsulated the complex intersections of wealth, power, personal sacrifice, and identity, all under the scrutiny of the public eye. This record-breaking sum was not just the result of a divorce; it was a reflection of years of personal, emotional, and legal struggles, as well as the cost of a life lived in the shadow of immense wealth.

Jocelyn Wildenstein's marriage to Alec Wildenstein, heir to one of the wealthiest and most influential art-dealing families in the world, had begun with great promise. Alec's family fortune was built on a legacy of fine art, lucrative investments, and powerful social connections, making him one of the wealthiest men in France and the United States. For Jocelyn, the marriage represented an escape from her relatively modest beginnings in Switzerland, a chance to embrace the glittering world of high society and luxury.

In the early years of their marriage, Jocelyn became the quintessential trophy wife. Living in opulent estates in Paris, New York, and beyond, she was expected to maintain a perfect image of elegance and grace, fulfilling her role as Alec's social partner. Over time, however, Jocelyn's identity began to shift.

The demands of her marriage, particularly the emotional neglect she often faced from Alec, led her to dedicate herself more and more to ensuring her personal appearance aligned with her husband's status. Her extensive and often controversial cosmetic surgeries, including facial alterations that later earned her the nickname "Catwoman," became one of the hallmarks of her public identity.

Jocelyn, however, was not just a passive figure in her marriage. She had sacrificed much of her own career aspirations and personal interests to support Alec's business endeavors and to help nurture the Wildenstein family's legacy. She devoted herself to maintaining the social image and public persona that Alec's wealth and status required, often at the cost of her emotional and mental well-being. When Alec's infidelity came to light and the cracks in their marriage deepened, Jocelyn's decision to fight for a large financial settlement was not only about securing her future but also about recognizing the sacrifices she had made throughout the years.

When Jocelyn filed for divorce in 1999, the public was initially shocked by the scale of her demands. Her legal team reportedly sought a sum that would match the lifestyle she had become accustomed to an extravagant sum that would ensure she continued to live a life of unparalleled luxury. The figure that Jocelyn and her lawyers set was an eye-watering $2.5 billion. This included a cash settlement, a substantial share of Alec's real estate portfolio, and a portion of the family's valuable art collection, which was estimated to be worth billions of dollars.

At the core of Jocelyn's demands was her belief that she had, over the years, contributed significantly to Alec's wealth and success. Her role in maintaining the Wildenstein family's public image, particularly in the art world and high society, was crucial. In Jocelyn's view, she had sacrificed her own dreams, career aspirations, and personal interests to be the supportive wife that Alec required, and now, with the marriage dissolved, it was time for her to be compensated for those sacrifices.

Moreover, Jocelyn felt that her requests were justified by the nature of her emotional investment in the marriage. She had dedicated herself to Alec's well-being and success, even as their relationship became more strained.

The public revelation of Alec's infidelity further exacerbated Jocelyn's sense of betrayal, and the divorce became, in part, a means of asserting her worth and securing a future that would not leave her destitute. The $2.5 billion sum, while seemingly exorbitant, represented both her financial needs and an acknowledgment of the years of emotional turmoil she had endured.

The divorce battle between Jocelyn and Alec Wildenstein quickly became a contentious and high-profile affair, with both sides fiercely fighting for control of the financial outcomes. Alec, who was fiercely protective of his family's wealth and legacy, refused to give in to Jocelyn's demands without a fight.

His legal team argued that Jocelyn's request for such a large settlement was excessive, especially given the considerable assets she had already received during their marriage. Alec's side also sought to portray her demands as unrealistic and rooted in her desire for revenge after the emotional betrayal of his infidelity.

In contrast, Jocelyn's legal team worked tirelessly to present her case in a way that justified the astronomical amount she was requesting. They emphasized the sacrifices she had made over the years, particularly the emotional toll of Alec's infidelity, his distant behavior, and her commitment to their marriage at the expense of her own personal and professional development. In their eyes, the $2.5 billion settlement was not a mere financial windfall, but a reflection of the immense contributions Jocelyn had made to Alec's life, both personally and professionally.

At the heart of the dispute was not just the money, but the future of the Wildenstein family empire. The vast wealth at stake included valuable real estate holdings, priceless works of art, and the family's significant influence in the art world. The divorce proceedings thus became a battle not just over a couple's personal assets but over the control of one of the world's largest art fortunes.

While the divorce proceedings were taking place in the courts, the media was covering every development with intense interest. The Wildenstein family's wealth and status had already made them the subject of public fascination, but the acrimonious divorce turned the spotlight on Jocelyn and Alec in a way that few could have predicted.

Jocelyn's appearance, particularly her highly publicized cosmetic surgeries, was a frequent topic of discussion, with tabloids gleefully dubbing her "Catwoman" and scrutinizing her every physical transformation. The media turned her into a symbol of vanity, wealth, and obsession, overshadowing the deeper emotional and financial aspects of the divorce.

For Jocelyn, the media's portrayal of her as a woman obsessed with beauty and wealth only compounded the difficulties she faced in her personal life. The public scrutiny of her physical appearance became one of the focal points of the divorce trial. Every detail of her transformation, both physical and emotional, was laid bare for the world to see.

The press often ridiculed her for her surgeries, ignoring the underlying pain and sacrifice that motivated her decisions. The media narrative, which often painted Jocelyn as a woman who had used her beauty to manipulate her husband, overlooked the more nuanced reality of her marriage, where emotional neglect and betrayal played a significant role.

After years of legal wrangling, the Wildenstein divorce was finally settled in 1999, with Jocelyn being awarded a staggering $2.5 billion. This sum, which included a combination of cash, real estate, and assets from Alec's art collection, made it one of the largest divorce settlements in history. While the exact details of the settlement were never fully disclosed, the reported figure was jaw-dropping, particularly in comparison to other celebrity divorces at the time.

For Jocelyn, the settlement was a bittersweet victory. While she had secured financial security for herself, the settlement could not undo the emotional and psychological damage that had been done over the years. Her identity, once so tied to her marriage to Alec, had been severely altered by the public nature of the divorce, and the media's portrayal of her had left lasting scars. The money, while vast, could not replace the years of pain and emotional neglect that had characterized her marriage.

The settlement also marked the end of a significant chapter in the Wildenstein family's history. Alec, despite retaining a large portion of the family's fortune, had been forced to give up a significant amount of his wealth, and the Wildenstein name was forever linked to the public spectacle of the divorce. The financial impact was far-reaching, not just for the Wildensteins, but for the art world and the broader circles of wealth and influence they had once dominated.

In the years following the divorce, Jocelyn continued to live a life of luxury, thanks to the massive settlement. She invested her money wisely, maintaining a lifestyle that reflected her former status as Alec Wildenstein's wife. However, her public image was forever tainted by the media's portrayal of her as a woman driven by vanity and financial gain. Despite her efforts to move beyond the divorce, she remained a subject of fascination for the tabloids, who continued to scrutinize her every move.

For Alec, the divorce marked a loss not only of wealth but also of reputation. The public nature of the divorce and the media frenzy surrounding his affair and the settlement left a lasting mark on his legacy. His personal and professional life would never fully recover from the fallout of the trial.

Ultimately, Jocelyn's record-breaking settlement represented both a financial triumph and a personal tragedy. The immense sum secured her future, but it came at the cost of her public reputation and emotional well-being. The divorce was a painful reminder that even the greatest wealth cannot shield one from emotional suffering, and that the price of a gilded life is often higher than anyone could anticipate.

10.2 Lingering Scars from a Publicized Breakup

The breakup between Jocelyn and Alec Wildenstein, which unfolded in the glare of public scrutiny, left emotional and psychological scars that would linger long after the legal proceedings were over. For both Jocelyn and Alec, the media frenzy surrounding their divorce trial and the way their personal lives were exposed to the public eye caused irreparable damage to their reputations, identities, and mental well-being.

The public nature of the divorce, combined with its sensational elements, including Jocelyn's extensive cosmetic surgeries and Alec's infidelity, created a toxic environment in which both individuals were forced to confront not only the collapse of their marriage but also the harsh judgments and invasive scrutiny of the public.

Jocelyn, in particular, faced the brunt of the media's scorn, with her appearance and personal life becoming the subject of ridicule. The scars from the publicized breakup were not merely financial but deeply emotional. She found herself portrayed as a woman obsessed with beauty and wealth, overshadowing her years of sacrifice in the marriage and the emotional toll that had led to the eventual divorce. The pain of this publicized breakdown of her marriage, combined with the emotional neglect and infidelity she experienced within it, would remain with her for years to come.

The most immediate consequence of the publicized divorce was the damage to Jocelyn Wildenstein's personal identity. Jocelyn had built much of her life and image around her marriage to Alec, and with the divorce came a loss of the public persona that had defined her for years.

While she had once been seen as a glamorous, wealthy socialite married to one of the world's most powerful men, her identity in the public eye soon became defined by the dramatic transformation she underwent through cosmetic surgeries. Her appearance, which had become increasingly feline-like over the years, was a focal point for the media, turning her into a symbol of vanity, obsession, and excess.

The tabloids, eager for sensational stories, christened her with the infamous nickname "Catwoman." This label, which emphasized her physical transformation, eclipsed any focus on her character or the reasons behind her surgeries. Rather than being viewed as a woman who had endured emotional neglect, infidelity, and personal sacrifices throughout her marriage, Jocelyn became a punchline in a public spectacle.

She was depicted as a woman who sought to change her appearance in order to maintain her husband's affection, reinforcing the idea that her obsession with beauty and youth was her defining characteristic. This superficial portrayal of Jocelyn ignored the more profound emotional aspects of her story, leaving her with a fractured sense of self and a public identity that was almost entirely defined by her appearance.

The emotional scars of this humiliation were deep. It was not just about the media's criticism of her cosmetic surgeries, it was about the way her entire identity had been stripped away and replaced with a label that she could not escape. The public ridicule took a heavy toll on Jocelyn's self-esteem. Instead of being celebrated for the person she was, she was relentlessly criticized and reduced to a caricature. As her physical transformation continued, the media only intensified their focus on her appearance, making it harder for Jocelyn to regain a sense of normalcy or control over her public persona.

Jocelyn's divorce from Alec left her emotionally shattered. The breakdown of their marriage had been long in the making, but the emotional toll was amplified by the public nature of the divorce. Alec's infidelity had been one of the key factors that pushed Jocelyn to file for divorce, but the media coverage made it seem as though Jocelyn's pain was less about betrayal and more about her obsession with securing wealth and maintaining her appearance. The emotional and personal anguish she had endured in the marriage was minimized or ignored by the media, which instead focused on the superficial aspects of the case.

This public betrayal, coupled with the media's constant intrusion into her life, left Jocelyn feeling isolated and vulnerable. Her emotional wounds from the marriage, and the subsequent divorce, were compounded by the sense of humiliation and loneliness that accompanied the media's relentless scrutiny.

In the years following the divorce, Jocelyn would continue to grapple with these emotional scars. The overwhelming sense of isolation she felt from both her former husband and the public was not easily overcome. Despite the immense financial settlement she received, it was clear that the personal price she paid was far greater than the wealth she had secured.

The public's judgment of Jocelyn as a superficial, beauty-obsessed woman obscured the deeper emotional struggles she faced. Her loneliness intensified as she realized that the world saw her as a symbol of excess and vanity, ignoring the fact that she had been a woman who had loved her husband and devoted herself to a life that she believed was built on mutual respect and affection. The emotional toll of the divorce was far-reaching, and the lingering scars would shape her future relationships and her sense of self-worth.

Following her divorce from Alec, Jocelyn faced significant difficulties in establishing new relationships. The emotional scars from her marriage, coupled with the public nature of her divorce, made it difficult for her to trust others. She had been betrayed by the man she had loved and invested so much in, and the subsequent public humiliation only deepened her sense of distrust. The idea of opening up to another person, let alone entering into a new relationship, seemed daunting to Jocelyn. She had already given so much of herself to a marriage that ultimately ended in betrayal and disgrace.

Furthermore, her personal life was often the subject of public speculation. Tabloid reports continued to track her every move, and her relationships, or perceived lack thereof, became the fodder for gossip columns. For someone who had been used to a certain level of intimacy in her marriage, the invasion of her privacy in the aftermath of her divorce was both alienating and painful. She was constantly reminded of the public judgment and the lingering stigma attached to her image.

Trust, which had been shattered in her marriage, was not easily rebuilt. The emotional vulnerability she experienced throughout her relationship with Alec made it difficult for her to feel secure in her own skin, and the media's constant portrayal of her as a woman obsessed with appearance only made her feel more disconnected from her true self. The lingering scars from her marriage and divorce impacted her ability to trust not only potential partners but also friends and acquaintances who continued to judge her based on the public persona that had been crafted for her.

While Jocelyn's $2.5 billion divorce settlement was one of the largest in history, the financial windfall did little to mitigate the emotional costs of her divorce. The settlement ensured that Jocelyn would never have to worry about money again, but it could not replace the emotional security and stability she had lost in her marriage. It was a painful reminder that money, no matter how vast, cannot heal wounds of the heart.

Jocelyn's wealth allowed her to continue living a life of luxury, but it did not bring her the peace of mind she so desperately sought. The years of emotional neglect, betrayal, and public ridicule left deep scars that no amount of money could erase. The financial settlement, while securing her future, became a constant reminder of the sacrifices she had made during her marriage, sacrifices that had not been appreciated or reciprocated. Despite the vast sum she had won in the divorce, the emotional toll of her broken marriage and the public fallout continued to affect her in ways that money could not solve.

Perhaps the most enduring scar from Jocelyn's publicized divorce is the "Catwoman" persona that the media cemented for her. Over the years, the media's portrayal of Jocelyn as a beauty-obsessed, vain woman who had transformed herself physically in pursuit of Alec's affection overshadowed the more nuanced aspects of her story. This caricatured image of Jocelyn as a woman obsessed with perfection and wealth became inextricably linked to her identity, and it was a narrative that Jocelyn found herself unable to escape.

The "Catwoman" nickname, which initially was a taunt, became the central feature of her public identity. Despite her efforts to rebuild her life and move beyond the trauma of the divorce, the media continued to focus on her appearance and her past. The constant reminders of the divorce, coupled with the public scrutiny of her appearance, made it difficult for Jocelyn to establish a new sense of self outside the legacy of her marriage and the subsequent divorce.

As years passed, the "Catwoman" label became a symbol of both Jocelyn's personal transformation and her public humiliation. Despite her immense wealth and the financial independence she had achieved through the settlement, she remained tethered to the public persona created by the media. The emotional scars from the public breakup were thus not just psychological but also deeply intertwined with her public image, making it difficult for Jocelyn to ever fully escape the shadows of her past.

In the aftermath of her divorce, Jocelyn Wildenstein's life was forever altered. The emotional scars from the publicized breakup were multifaceted: a shattered sense of self, the constant barrage of media criticism, loneliness, and the pain of betrayal.

While the billion-dollar settlement provided financial security, it could not undo the damage that had been done to her identity, her sense of worth, and her emotional well-being. The public nature of her divorce, the relentless media scrutiny, the tabloid gossip, and the judgmental portrayal of her appearance, left Jocelyn to wrestle with an image that she could not escape.

Her story is a stark reminder that, for some, the price of a high-profile breakup can extend far beyond financial compensation. The scars left behind are often not visible in the form of wealth, but in the deep, lingering emotional wounds that can take years, if not a lifetime, to heal.

CHAPTER ELEVEN: FROM HEIRESS TO BANKRUPTCY

Jocelyn Wildenstein's life has been one of dramatic highs and lows, and few chapters illustrate this better than her journey from the extravagant wealth of an heiress to the stark reality of bankruptcy. Known globally as the recipient of one of the largest divorce settlements in history, a reported $2.5 billion from her ex-husband Alec Wildenstein, Jocelyn's financial decline serves as a cautionary tale about the fleeting nature of wealth, the complexities of managing money, and the emotional toll of public scrutiny.

The descent from her lavish lifestyle to declaring bankruptcy in 2018 shocked many. It exposed the challenges of maintaining immense wealth while grappling with personal struggles, legal disputes, and the mounting cost of living a life that was once subsidized by unimaginable riches. Jocelyn's story of financial collapse is not just about money, it is a narrative of identity, survival, and reinvention in the face of adversity.

During her marriage to Alec Wildenstein, Jocelyn lived a life that few could imagine. Together, the couple owned sprawling estates, private jets, luxury yachts, and one of the world's most significant art collections. Their properties ranged from the extravagant Wildenstein townhouse in Manhattan to a palatial estate in Kenya. They hosted lavish parties, rubbed shoulders with the elite, and moved in circles of extraordinary privilege.

After her divorce in 1999, Jocelyn retained a significant share of this wealth. Her settlement included an immediate $2.5 billion payout, followed by annual payments of $100 million for the next 13 years. It was a staggering sum, ensuring her a lifetime of financial independence, or so it seemed.

Jocelyn continued to live in the manner she had become accustomed to, maintaining residences in Manhattan and elsewhere, traveling extensively, and indulging her love for couture fashion and exotic pets. However, maintaining this lifestyle came at a high cost, one that eventually became unsustainable.

While Jocelyn was financially well-off after her divorce, her spending habits and the high costs of her lifestyle quickly began to erode her fortune. Reports suggest that Jocelyn spent extravagantly on maintaining her Manhattan residence, hosting opulent social events, and traveling in private jets. Her taste for luxury extended to everything she did, from dining to fashion, and she reportedly spent millions on her prized pets, including rare birds and wild cats.

Additionally, Jocelyn's passion for cosmetic surgery was another significant financial drain. Over the years, she underwent numerous procedures to maintain and enhance her appearance, which many speculated were aimed at achieving a feline-like visage inspired by her love for big cats. These surgeries, often criticized by the media, were not only costly but also fueled public fascination and ridicule.

Despite her substantial settlement, Jocelyn's expenses far outpaced her income. By the time the annual payments from her divorce settlement ceased in 2012, her financial situation had already begun to show signs of strain. Without the structured payouts, Jocelyn was left to rely solely on the fortune she had amassed, a fortune that was rapidly diminishing.

Jocelyn's financial troubles were compounded by a series of legal disputes and financial mismanagement. Over the years, she faced lawsuits from creditors and landlords, who claimed that she had failed to pay her bills. In 2013, she was sued by her former New York City landlord for owing more than $70,000 in unpaid rent on her luxury apartment. Similar lawsuits followed, with Jocelyn reportedly defaulting on payments for services ranging from personal security to luxury goods.

Her legal troubles extended beyond financial disputes. Jocelyn's tumultuous personal relationships also contributed to her financial decline. She faced allegations of domestic disputes with her fiancé, Lloyd Klein, which led to legal battles that further drained her resources. These incidents, combined with ongoing public scrutiny, created a perfect storm of financial and emotional strain.

In May 2018, Jocelyn Wildenstein made headlines once again, but this time, it was not for her opulent lifestyle or high-profile relationships. She filed for Chapter 11 bankruptcy in a Manhattan court, listing her assets and liabilities in legal documents that painted a stark picture of her financial downfall. According to the filings, Jocelyn claimed to have no steady income and listed her monthly expenses at over $25,000, far exceeding her reported income of $0.

The bankruptcy documents revealed that Jocelyn owed millions of dollars to creditors, including unpaid legal fees, credit card debt, and overdue rent. Among her listed debts were over $4.6 million to various creditors and $175,000 owed to a storage company for holding her personal belongings. These figures were a far cry from the vast wealth she had once controlled, and they shocked many who had assumed her divorce settlement had ensured her lifelong financial stability.

The bankruptcy filing marked a dramatic fall from grace for a woman who had once been one of the wealthiest divorcees in the world. It was a sobering reminder that even immense wealth can be fleeting without careful management and planning.

Jocelyn's financial troubles were not just a matter of numbers, they also took a significant emotional toll on her. For a woman who had spent decades living a life of extraordinary luxury and privilege, the experience of financial insecurity was deeply unsettling. The public nature of her bankruptcy filing only added to the humiliation, as media outlets around the world covered the story with a mix of fascination and schadenfreude.

The loss of her financial independence also forced Jocelyn to confront the reality of her life post-divorce. While she had once been a glamorous socialite at the center of New York's elite circles, her financial decline made it increasingly difficult for her to maintain the same level of social engagement. Her diminished resources, combined with the public ridicule she faced, left her feeling isolated and vulnerable.

Jocelyn Wildenstein's journey from heiress to bankruptcy is a stark reminder of the complexities of wealth and the importance of financial planning. Despite her substantial divorce settlement, Jocelyn's story highlights how even immense fortunes can be eroded by overspending, legal troubles, and the high cost of maintaining an extravagant lifestyle. Her financial collapse underscores the need for sustainable wealth management, particularly for those accustomed to a life of privilege.

At the same time, Jocelyn's experience also speaks to the emotional challenges of wealth and public scrutiny. Her identity, once tied to her marriage and social status, was fundamentally altered by her divorce and financial troubles. The public fascination with her life, fueled by her dramatic transformation and high-profile relationships, only added to the pressure she faced as she struggled to rebuild her life.

Despite the challenges she has faced, Jocelyn Wildenstein's story is not just one of loss but also of resilience. Her ability to confront the realities of her financial situation and take steps to address them, including filing for bankruptcy, demonstrates her determination to move forward. While the road to financial recovery may be long, Jocelyn's story is a testament to the human capacity for reinvention and survival in the face of adversity.

As Jocelyn continues to navigate the complexities of her life post-bankruptcy, her story serves as a powerful reminder of the pitfalls of wealth and the importance of maintaining a balance between material success and emotional well-being. For those who followed her journey from heiress to bankruptcy, her life remains a compelling narrative of triumphs, trials, and the enduring quest for identity and stability.

11.1 Financial Troubles and Extravagant Spending

Jocelyn Wildenstein's life is a case study in the perils of excessive spending and financial mismanagement, even in the face of seemingly limitless wealth. Known for her opulent lifestyle and one of the largest divorce settlements in history, Jocelyn's financial troubles have captivated public attention for decades. Her journey from unimaginable wealth to bankruptcy reveals the dangers of living beyond one's means and the consequences of neglecting financial discipline.

Jocelyn's financial troubles began long before her infamous bankruptcy filing. Her marriage to Alec Wildenstein, a billionaire art dealer and heir to a family fortune, introduced her to a lifestyle of unprecedented luxury. The couple lived in a lavish townhouse in Manhattan, owned sprawling estates, and traveled the world aboard private jets and luxury yachts. Their social calendar was filled with exclusive parties, and their passion for exotic pets added another layer of extravagance to their lives.

After their divorce in 1999, Jocelyn was awarded a record-breaking $2.5 billion settlement, with an additional $100 million annually for 13 years. This staggering sum placed her among the wealthiest women in the world, seemingly ensuring her financial security for life. However, this fortune would prove insufficient to sustain her extravagant lifestyle, as Jocelyn continued to spend at a rate that far outpaced her income.

Jocelyn's spending habits reflected her commitment to maintaining the luxurious lifestyle she had enjoyed during her marriage. Her expenses included:

1. Real Estate: Jocelyn retained the couple's Manhattan townhouse, a multi-million-dollar property that required substantial upkeep. She also owned other residences, each with its own high maintenance costs.

2. Fashion and Jewelry: Known for her love of haute couture, Jocelyn spent millions on designer clothing, accessories, and custom jewelry. Her wardrobe was a testament to her devotion to luxury and style.

3. Travel: Private jets and first-class accommodations were the norm for Jocelyn. She traveled extensively, often staying in the world's most exclusive hotels and resorts.

4. Pets and Exotic Animals: Jocelyn's love for exotic pets, including big cats, was well-documented. She spent considerable sums on their care, including specialized enclosures and veterinary services.

5. Cosmetic Surgery: Jocelyn's numerous cosmetic surgeries to achieve her iconic feline-like appearance were another significant expense. These procedures were not only costly but also required ongoing maintenance and recovery.

Jocelyn's lavish spending was not without consequences. The costs associated with her lifestyle began to mount, and as her annual divorce payments ended in 2012, the financial strain became apparent. Without the steady influx of funds, Jocelyn was left to rely on the fortune she had amassed, which was rapidly dwindling.

Her financial troubles were exacerbated by her inability, or unwillingness, to adjust her spending habits. Jocelyn continued to live as if her resources were infinite, ignoring the reality that even a multi-billion-dollar fortune could be depleted. This disconnect between her income and expenses set the stage for her eventual bankruptcy.

As her financial situation deteriorated, Jocelyn faced a series of legal battles that further drained her resources. Landlords, creditors, and service providers sued her for unpaid bills, painting a picture of a woman struggling to maintain her opulent lifestyle.

1. Unpaid Rent: In 2013, Jocelyn was sued by her Manhattan landlord for failing to pay over $70,000 in rent on her luxury apartment. Similar disputes followed, with reports of overdue payments and legal judgments against her.

2. Credit Card Debt: Jocelyn accumulated significant credit card debt, further straining her finances. She reportedly owed substantial sums to multiple creditors.

3. Legal Fees: The cost of defending herself in numerous lawsuits added to Jocelyn's financial woes. Legal battles over her personal life and financial obligations drained what remained of her wealth.

By 2018, Jocelyn's financial troubles had reached a breaking point. She filed for Chapter 11 bankruptcy in a Manhattan court, listing her assets and liabilities in legal documents that revealed the extent of her financial decline. According to the filings:

Jocelyn claimed no steady income and reported monthly expenses of over $25,000, with no means to cover them. She listed debts of over $4.6 million, including overdue rent, legal fees, and credit card balances. Her assets, once valued in the billions, had dwindled significantly, leaving her unable to meet her financial obligations.

The bankruptcy filing was a stark contrast to the life of unimaginable wealth Jocelyn had once enjoyed. It marked the culmination of years of extravagant spending, financial mismanagement, and the challenges of sustaining a high-profile lifestyle without adequate resources.

For Jocelyn, the financial strain was not just a matter of dollars and cents. The emotional toll of her declining wealth and public bankruptcy filing was immense. Once celebrated as a glamorous socialite, she became the subject of public ridicule and speculation. The media coverage of her financial troubles only added to her humiliation, as her personal struggles were laid bare for the world to see.

The loss of her financial independence also forced Jocelyn to confront deeper questions about her identity. For decades, her life had been defined by wealth, beauty, and social status. As her fortune dwindled, she was forced to grapple with the reality of a life that no longer aligned with the image she had cultivated.

Jocelyn Wildenstein's financial troubles offer valuable lessons about the importance of financial planning and the risks of excessive spending. Her story illustrates that even immense wealth can be fleeting without careful management and a clear understanding of one's financial limits. Key takeaways include:

Sustainable Wealth Management: Maintaining a fortune requires discipline and planning. Overspending, even on luxury items, can quickly erode even the largest bank accounts.

Adapting to Changing Circumstances: Jocelyn's failure to adjust her spending habits after her divorce payments ended was a critical factor in her financial decline. Adapting to new financial realities is essential for long-term stability.

Avoiding Public Scrutiny: The public nature of Jocelyn's financial troubles added to her challenges. Managing finances discreetly and proactively can help avoid unnecessary legal and personal issues.

Jocelyn Wildenstein's story is one of contrasts: unimaginable wealth and devastating financial struggles, public glamour and private turmoil. Her journey from heiress to bankruptcy serves as a cautionary tale about the dangers of excess and the importance of financial stewardship. While her life has been marked by dramatic highs and lows, Jocelyn's resilience and ability to adapt offer hope for a future where she can rebuild and redefine her legacy.

11.2 Navigating Life Without Alec's Fortune

Jocelyn Wildenstein's life after her divorce from Alec Wildenstein marked a turning point that required her to navigate a world vastly different from the one she had known during their marriage. While the divorce settlement provided her with an astronomical sum of money, the transition from being part of a shared, generational fortune to managing her finances independently proved to be an immense challenge. Her story is a complex narrative of resilience, missteps, and adaptation as she attempted to sustain the glamorous lifestyle she had grown accustomed to.

The 1999 divorce settlement awarded Jocelyn $2.5 billion upfront and an additional $100 million annually for 13 years, a total sum of $3.8 billion. At the time, it was one of the largest divorce settlements in history, and it cemented Jocelyn's reputation as a woman of extraordinary wealth.

However, this wealth came with significant strings attached. Jocelyn was reportedly prohibited from using any part of the settlement to fund plastic surgery, a condition that highlighted the tension surrounding her appearance and lifestyle. Despite this clause, Jocelyn continued to indulge her passion for cosmetic enhancements and other luxury expenditures.

The years following the divorce saw Jocelyn continuing to live in the manner she had during her marriage. She remained in the couple's opulent Manhattan townhouse, where she hosted extravagant parties and entertained members of high society. Her love for couture fashion and exotic pets endured, as did her penchant for frequent travel in private jets and stays in five-star hotels.

Jocelyn's lifestyle choices were not just a reflection of her wealth but also a statement of her identity. Having been a part of one of the most elite families in the world, she sought to maintain her place in high society. However, this relentless pursuit of luxury came at a significant financial cost, one that would eventually erode her vast fortune.

One of the critical challenges Jocelyn faced after her divorce was managing her finances independently. While she had access to extraordinary sums of money, her lack of financial discipline and reliance on lavish spending habits quickly created problems. Reports suggest that Jocelyn had little experience in handling money, as her lifestyle during her marriage was funded entirely by Alec's family fortune.

Her spending outpaced her income, even with the substantial annual payments from her divorce settlement. By 2012, when the structured payments ceased, Jocelyn was left with her remaining assets, a sum that had been significantly depleted by years of unchecked spending.

The cessation of her annual payments marked a turning point in Jocelyn's financial journey. No longer bolstered by Alec's fortune, she was forced to confront the reality of her dwindling resources. The once-limitless wealth that had sustained her lifestyle was now finite, and Jocelyn struggled to adapt.

1. Real Estate Costs: Maintaining her Manhattan townhouse became increasingly difficult as property taxes, maintenance costs, and other expenses mounted. She eventually faced legal disputes over unpaid rent and other property-related debts.

2. Legal Troubles: Jocelyn's financial troubles were compounded by a series of lawsuits from creditors and service providers. These legal battles drained her remaining resources and highlighted her inability to keep up with her financial obligations.

3. Public Scrutiny: As her financial struggles became public knowledge, Jocelyn faced intense media scrutiny. The public fascination with her appearance and lifestyle only intensified, adding emotional strain to her already precarious situation.

The loss of Alec's fortune was not just a financial blow but also an emotional and social one. Jocelyn's identity had long been tied to her role as a member of the Wildenstein family, and her wealth had been a key part of her status in society. Without Alec's fortune, Jocelyn found herself increasingly isolated from the circles she had once been a part of.

The public nature of her financial troubles added to her sense of vulnerability. Once celebrated as a glamorous socialite, she became the subject of ridicule and speculation. This shift in public perception was deeply painful for Jocelyn, as it forced her to confront a reality that no longer aligned with the image she had cultivated.

In 2018, Jocelyn filed for Chapter 11 bankruptcy, listing her assets and liabilities in court documents that revealed the full extent of her financial decline. The filing marked a dramatic fall from grace for a woman who had once been one of the wealthiest divorcees in the world. It was a sobering reminder of the challenges she faced in navigating life without Alec's fortune.

The bankruptcy filing was also an opportunity for Jocelyn to reassess her priorities and begin the process of rebuilding. While it was a deeply humbling experience, it forced her to confront the reality of her situation and take steps toward financial stability.

Despite the challenges she faced, Jocelyn's journey is also one of resilience. Her ability to endure public scrutiny, financial hardship, and personal loss speaks to her strength and determination. While she may no longer enjoy the same level of wealth and privilege, Jocelyn's story is a testament to the human capacity for adaptation and reinvention.

As Jocelyn continues to navigate life without Alec's fortune, she remains a complex and fascinating figure. Her experiences serve as both a cautionary tale and a source of inspiration, highlighting the importance of financial planning, emotional resilience, and the power of reinvention. In the end, Jocelyn's life is a reminder that true wealth lies not in material possessions but in the ability to overcome adversity and find meaning in the face of change.

CHAPTER TWELVE: FACING THE CRITICS

Jocelyn Wildenstein's life has been a perpetual dance under the glare of an unrelenting spotlight, where her every move, decision, and transformation have been scrutinized, dissected, and debated. From her rise to prominence as a socialite and her tumultuous marriage to Alec Wildenstein, to the dramatic physical changes that redefined her public persona, Jocelyn became a lightning rod for criticism. While many admired her resilience and boldness, others used her as a symbol of excess, judgment often delivered with little regard for the nuances of her life or her personal struggles.

The media played a significant role in amplifying the criticism surrounding Jocelyn. Her divorce from Alec, one of the most publicized and expensive in history, turned her into a global spectacle. Tabloids pounced on the staggering $2.5 billion settlement and $100 million annual payments, painting her as a caricature of extravagance.

However, it was her appearance that dominated headlines. Jocelyn's love for cosmetic surgery, driven by her desire to embody feline-like features, became fodder for ridicule. The press dubbed her "Catwoman," a moniker that stuck and became shorthand for extreme beauty standards and perceived vanity. This label, while sensational and profitable for tabloids, was deeply dehumanizing for Jocelyn, reducing her identity to a single facet of her complex life.

Beyond the media frenzy, Jocelyn faced the judgment of society at large. Her transformation challenged conventional standards of beauty and provoked discomfort among those who valued conformity over individuality. For many, her surgeries represented an excess of privilege, a woman who could afford to reshape herself entirely, yet chose to do so in a way that defied traditional aesthetics.

This critique was layered with gendered assumptions. As a woman, Jocelyn's choices were scrutinized more harshly, her autonomy over her body framed as recklessness or insecurity rather than empowerment. Public perception rarely afforded her the grace to be seen as someone exercising personal agency in a deeply personal matter.

Compounding the external criticism was the tension within her personal relationships. Alec Wildenstein's family, deeply rooted in a culture of discretion and tradition, reportedly disapproved of Jocelyn's lifestyle and her physical transformation. Their disapproval further isolated her and fueled public narratives of a woman out of step with the world she married into.

Friends from her social circle, once eager to bask in the glow of her lavish lifestyle, began to distance themselves as her controversies mounted. This social ostracization was perhaps the most painful criticism of all, a reminder that wealth and fame often come with conditional acceptance.

Even in the face of such pervasive critique, Jocelyn remained defiant. She rarely bowed to public opinion or attempted to conform to societal expectations. Her determination to live life on her own terms, regardless of the cost, was a testament to her resilience. While the criticism undoubtedly left scars, Jocelyn's refusal to apologize for her choices spoke to an inner strength that many failed to recognize.

The digital age only intensified the scrutiny. Memes and viral content turned Jocelyn's life into a punchline, her image shared across social media platforms as a symbol of excess and spectacle. This shift from traditional media to internet ridicule brought a new wave of challenges, as the anonymity of the online world emboldened critics to be even harsher. Yet, Jocelyn continued to navigate this uncharted territory with the same resolve, understanding that the world's fascination with her said more about society's obsession with beauty, wealth, and fame than it did about her as a person.

Ultimately, Jocelyn Wildenstein's journey of facing the critics is a complex narrative of vulnerability and strength. She endured relentless judgment, not only for her choices but for the life she dared to live unapologetically. Her story serves as both a cautionary tale and a reflection of society's fascination with, and condemnation of, those who defy convention. Through it all, Jocelyn remains a symbol of resilience, a reminder that even under the harshest spotlight, the human spirit can persevere.

12.1 Coping with Ridicule and Media Scrutiny

Jocelyn Wildenstein's life has been a constant interplay of wealth, beauty, and public fascination. Yet, at the heart of her journey lies a struggle that is deeply personal: navigating the ridicule and media scrutiny that followed her every move. From her high-profile divorce to her dramatic physical transformation, Jocelyn became an object of intense curiosity and, often, mockery. Coping with this relentless attention required resilience, self-awareness, and an unyielding determination to define her identity beyond the headlines.

The media's obsession with Jocelyn began in earnest during her divorce from Alec Wildenstein, a case that became one of the most publicized legal battles of the late 20th century. The staggering figures of her settlement, $2.5 billion upfront and $100 million annually, catapulted her into the spotlight, making her a symbol of wealth and excess.

However, it was her physical appearance, more than her financial standing, that captured public attention. Jocelyn's love for cosmetic surgery, inspired by her fascination with feline aesthetics, became a focal point of media narratives. The press dubbed her "Catwoman," a nickname that quickly turned her into a global spectacle.

Ridicule came from all corners. Tabloid headlines mocked her surgeries, portraying her as a cautionary tale of vanity and excess. Late-night talk shows and comedians often used her as the butt of jokes, reducing her complex story to a punchline. Social media further amplified this ridicule, with memes and viral posts caricaturing her image and turning her into a subject of widespread mockery. For Jocelyn, this constant stream of criticism was not just a public challenge but a deeply personal affront to her sense of self.

One of the ways Jocelyn coped with this ridicule was by cultivating a sense of detachment from public opinion. She rarely gave interviews or responded to negative press, understanding that engaging with her critics would only fuel their narratives. Instead, she chose to focus on her personal passions and interests, such as art, fashion, and her love for exotic animals. By immersing herself in the things that brought her joy, she found a way to maintain a sense of normalcy amid the chaos of public scrutiny.

Her unwavering confidence also played a significant role in her ability to cope. Despite the criticism, Jocelyn never apologized for her choices or tried to conform to societal expectations. Her surgeries, she often said, were a reflection of her personal vision of beauty and not an attempt to meet anyone else's standards. This defiance was a powerful statement, a reminder that she was not defined by the opinions of others but by her own sense of self-worth.

Support from her inner circle was another crucial factor in her resilience. While many friends and acquaintances distanced themselves during her most controversial years, Jocelyn maintained close relationships with a select few who understood and supported her. These relationships provided her with a sanctuary from the outside world, a space where she could be herself without fear of judgment.

Jocelyn also found strength in her ability to adapt. As the nature of media scrutiny evolved, from tabloid stories to the instantaneous and often cruel world of social media, she learned to navigate these new challenges. She became more private, limiting her public appearances and sharing less about her personal life. This strategic retreat allowed her to reclaim some control over her narrative, even as public fascination with her story continued.

Coping with ridicule and media scrutiny is never easy, particularly for someone as high-profile as Jocelyn Wildenstein. Yet, her story is one of remarkable resilience. She endured decades of criticism, often tinged with misogyny and prejudice, and emerged with her dignity intact. While the world may have viewed her as a symbol of excess and spectacle, Jocelyn saw herself as an individual with the right to live life on her own terms.

Her journey offers a powerful lesson about the human spirit's capacity to withstand adversity. Jocelyn's ability to cope with ridicule and media scrutiny is not just a testament to her personal strength but also a critique of a society that is quick to judge and slow to empathize. Through it all, she has remained unapologetically herself, a woman who has faced the harshest of public judgments and chosen, time and again, to rise above them.

12.2 Advocacy for Self-Expression and Body Autonomy

Jocelyn Wildenstein's life has been a testament to the power and complexity of self-expression and body autonomy. As a woman who redefined beauty standards on her own terms, she became an emblem of the right to shape one's identity in defiance of societal expectations. Though her journey was often met with ridicule and criticism, it also opened up conversations about personal agency, the evolving concept of beauty, and the importance of body autonomy.

At the core of Jocelyn's advocacy for self-expression was her belief in the right to make decisions about one's body without external judgment. Her transformative journey through cosmetic surgery was not an impulsive pursuit but rather a deliberate and deeply personal choice.

Inspired by her admiration for feline aesthetics, Jocelyn sought to reflect a vision of beauty that resonated with her sense of self. While her choices were unconventional, they were hers alone—a bold assertion of her autonomy in a world that often pressures individuals, especially women, to conform to traditional standards.

Her story challenges societal norms around beauty and highlights the double standards that women face in expressing themselves. For centuries, women have been subjected to rigid beauty ideals that dictate how they should look, behave, and age.

Jocelyn's unapologetic embrace of cosmetic surgery pushed back against these norms, forcing society to confront its discomfort with individuals who defy expectations. Her choices sparked debates about what it means to be beautiful and whether society has the right to dictate the limits of personal transformation.

Jocelyn's life also underscores the importance of body autonomy as a fundamental human right. In a world where individuals are constantly judged for their appearances, Jocelyn's story reminds us that the body is a personal canvas, and each person has the right to shape it as they see fit. Her surgeries were not about pleasing others or adhering to societal standards but about expressing her unique identity. This perspective aligns with broader movements advocating for body positivity and the freedom to choose how one presents themselves to the world.

While Jocelyn never explicitly positioned herself as an advocate, her life became a case study in the complexities of self-expression. By standing firm in her choices despite widespread criticism, she inadvertently championed the idea that personal agency is more important than societal approval. Her resilience in the face of public scrutiny demonstrated the strength it takes to live authentically, even when the world disagrees with your vision.

Her journey also speaks to the broader cultural shifts surrounding body autonomy and cosmetic surgery. In recent years, society has become more accepting of individuals who choose to alter their appearances, whether through makeup, tattoos, or surgery. Jocelyn's story, though polarizing, contributed to these changing attitudes by challenging the stigma around cosmetic procedures and encouraging conversations about the right to self-expression.

Moreover, Jocelyn's life raises important questions about the intersection of wealth, privilege, and body autonomy. While her access to resources allowed her to explore avenues of self-expression that may not be available to everyone, it also subjected her to heightened scrutiny. Her story serves as a reminder that the right to self-expression should not be limited by socioeconomic status and that everyone deserves the freedom to make choices about their own bodies.

Advocacy for self-expression and body autonomy is about more than personal transformation, it is about the broader fight for acceptance and respect for individual choices. Jocelyn Wildenstein's life, with all its complexities, serves as a powerful narrative in this ongoing conversation. Her boldness in embracing her unique vision of beauty, despite societal pushback, reminds us of the importance of authenticity and the right to live on one's own terms.

In a world that is increasingly embracing diversity in appearance and identity, Jocelyn's story is a reminder that true self-expression requires courage and a deep commitment to one's sense of self. By living unapologetically, she not only claimed her own body autonomy but also paved the way for others to do the same, challenging a world that often seeks to limit individuality. Her legacy, whether viewed through the lens of admiration or critique, is a powerful call to celebrate and protect the freedom of self-expression for all.

CHAPTER THIRTEEN: REINVENTION AND RESILIENCE

Jocelyn Wildenstein's life story is one of remarkable reinvention and resilience, marked by her ability to adapt, endure, and redefine herself in the face of adversity. From her modest beginnings in Switzerland to her ascent into the echelons of global high society, and later through her very public trials and triumphs, Jocelyn's journey has been anything but ordinary. Her ability to confront challenges with determination and to reinvent herself repeatedly underscores the indomitable strength of her character.

Reinvention, for Jocelyn, was not merely an act of survival but a deliberate choice to pursue a life of personal expression and fulfillment. Born in Lausanne, Switzerland, Jocelyn grew up far removed from the wealth and glamour that would later define her life.

Her early years were shaped by a strong desire to transcend the limitations of her small-town upbringing. Armed with ambition and an adventurous spirit, she sought opportunities that would take her beyond the confines of her origins, eventually immersing herself in a world of art, culture, and high society.

Her marriage to Alec Wildenstein represented a significant chapter of reinvention, as she transitioned from a relatively unknown figure into a celebrated socialite. Immersed in the Wildenstein family's world of art, wealth, and influence, Jocelyn embraced her new role with enthusiasm.

She became a prominent figure in Manhattan's elite circles, hosting extravagant parties, traveling the world, and indulging in a life of luxury. Yet, even as she enjoyed the spoils of wealth, Jocelyn maintained a strong sense of identity, often expressing herself in ways that defied convention and challenged societal norms.

Jocelyn's most famous, and polarizing, act of reinvention came through her physical transformation. Inspired by her love for exotic feline beauty, she underwent numerous cosmetic procedures to achieve a look that she felt best represented her unique vision of beauty. While her transformation was met with public ridicule, it was a deeply personal journey for Jocelyn.

It was not about conforming to societal standards but about embracing her individuality. Her surgeries became both a symbol of her autonomy and a lightning rod for criticism, but Jocelyn remained unapologetic, demonstrating a resilience that allowed her to stand firm in her choices.

Resilience became a defining trait as Jocelyn faced a series of challenges that could have easily overwhelmed anyone else. Her high-profile divorce from Alec Wildenstein was one of the most tumultuous periods of her life, involving allegations of infidelity, financial disputes, and intense media scrutiny. The divorce, which resulted in a record-breaking settlement, turned Jocelyn into a tabloid sensation. Yet, even as the world dissected her personal life, she managed to maintain her composure and dignity, navigating the public spectacle with grace.

The years following her divorce presented new challenges, particularly financial difficulties. Despite the substantial settlement she received, Jocelyn faced bankruptcy due to her extravagant lifestyle and legal battles. The loss of her fortune could have marked the end of her prominence, but Jocelyn proved once again that she was more than her wealth. She adjusted to her new reality, demonstrating an ability to adapt and persevere even in the face of significant setbacks.

Jocelyn's resilience extended beyond her personal and financial struggles to her ability to reclaim her narrative. While the media continued to focus on her appearance and controversies, Jocelyn chose to focus on the aspects of her life that brought her joy and fulfillment. Whether through her love of art, her passion for animals, or her enduring friendships, she found ways to rebuild her life on her own terms.

Her story of reinvention and resilience offers valuable lessons about the power of self-determination. Jocelyn Wildenstein's life is a testament to the idea that reinvention is not about erasing the past but about building on it to create a future that aligns with one's values and desires. Her resilience reminds us that challenges, no matter how overwhelming, can be met with strength and grace.

Ultimately, Jocelyn's journey is a celebration of the human spirit's capacity to adapt and endure. Through her reinventions, she demonstrated that life is not defined by the setbacks we face but by how we choose to respond to them. Jocelyn Wildenstein's story is a reminder that resilience and reinvention are not just survival mechanisms, they are acts of courage and expressions of hope for a better future.

13.1 Jocelyn's Quieter Life in Recent Years

In recent years, Jocelyn Wildenstein has retreated from the public spotlight, opting for a quieter, more private existence far removed from the lavish parties and media frenzy that once defined her life. While her past remains a topic of fascination for many, Jocelyn has focused on finding peace, rebuilding her life, and embracing a lifestyle that prioritizes privacy and simplicity over the glitz and glamour of her earlier years.

The transition to a quieter life has not been without its challenges. Jocelyn's financial difficulties, including a bankruptcy filing in 2018, marked a significant shift from her days of opulence. After decades of extravagant spending on luxury homes, yachts, private jets, and elaborate parties, her financial situation forced her to reassess her priorities.

Reports of unpaid bills and legal battles painted a picture of a woman grappling with the realities of life without the vast wealth she once enjoyed. However, these challenges also offered Jocelyn an opportunity to reinvent herself once again, this time as someone learning to navigate life with greater restraint and practicality.

A key aspect of Jocelyn's quieter life has been her focus on personal relationships. She has maintained a long-term relationship with Lloyd Klein, a fashion designer with whom she has shared a tumultuous yet enduring bond. Their partnership has been a source of both support and controversy, with publicized disputes and reconciliations adding complexity to their story. Despite the ups and downs, their relationship has provided Jocelyn with a sense of stability and companionship, underscoring the importance of human connection in her life.

Jocelyn has also taken steps to maintain her love for art and animals, two passions that have defined her life from an early age. Her affinity for exotic animals, particularly big cats, remains a significant part of her identity.

Though she no longer lives in the sprawling estates where she once housed these magnificent creatures, her enduring love for them speaks to her deep connection with nature and her appreciation for beauty in all its forms. Similarly, her appreciation for art continues to shape her worldview, reminding her of the creative spirit that has always driven her.

While Jocelyn's physical transformation remains a topic of public curiosity, she has largely stepped back from the media's gaze. This retreat has allowed her to reclaim some control over her narrative, shifting the focus from her appearance to her personal journey. By choosing to live on her own terms, she has found a sense of peace that eluded her during her years as a tabloid fixture.

Living a quieter life has also allowed Jocelyn to reflect on her past and the lessons it holds. She has endured public scrutiny, financial hardship, and personal loss, yet she has emerged with a remarkable resilience that continues to define her. Her story is not just one of survival but of a woman who has consistently adapted to life's challenges, finding ways to thrive in the face of adversity.

For Jocelyn, this period of quiet is not a retreat but a reclamation of her individuality. It is a time to focus on the things that matter most, relationships, passions, and personal growth. By stepping away from the spotlight, she has been able to find solace in simplicity, proving that even those who have lived extraordinary lives can find contentment in the ordinary.

Jocelyn's quieter life in recent years is a poignant reminder that reinvention is a lifelong process. While her earlier years were defined by grandeur and public attention, this chapter of her life is characterized by introspection, resilience, and the pursuit of inner peace. In many ways, it is the most profound reinvention of all, a testament to the enduring strength of a woman who has faced the highs and lows of life with grace and determination.

13.2 Reflections on Her Journey and Legacy

As Jocelyn Wildenstein reflects on her extraordinary life, she stands as a figure of intrigue, resilience, and controversy. Her journey has been one of transformation, emotional, physical, and social, marked by triumphs and trials that have made her a household name.

Despite the public scrutiny and personal challenges she has faced, Jocelyn's life offers a complex narrative about individuality, the cost of ambition, and the power of self-determination. Her legacy, though polarizing, continues to spark conversations about beauty, autonomy, and the societal expectations placed upon women.

Jocelyn's reflections likely begin with her early years in Lausanne, Switzerland, where her dreams of glamour and excitement took root. Growing up in modest surroundings, she yearned for a life far beyond the quiet confines of her hometown. Her journey from a small Swiss town to the opulent circles of Manhattan's high society is a testament to her ambition and drive. It reflects a determination to break free from societal constraints and chart a path that was uniquely her own.

Her marriage to Alec Wildenstein brought her into a world of unimaginable wealth and influence. Yet, as she looks back, Jocelyn would likely acknowledge that this chapter of her life was as challenging as it was glamorous. While she gained access to art, culture, and luxury, she also encountered the pressures and complexities of maintaining a public image in an elite social circle. Her role as a socialite and art patron brought her joy and purpose, but it also set the stage for the intense scrutiny that would later define her public life.

The decision to undergo extensive cosmetic surgery remains one of the most controversial aspects of Jocelyn's story. Inspired by her fascination with feline beauty, these procedures were deeply personal acts of self-expression. While her transformation attracted ridicule and sensationalist media coverage, Jocelyn stood by her choices, viewing them as an extension of her individuality. Reflecting on this, she may see her surgeries as a bold assertion of body autonomy, a declaration that beauty is subjective and deeply personal.

However, Jocelyn's journey was not without pain. Her divorce from Alec Wildenstein was a turning point that exposed her to public judgment on an unprecedented scale. The "billion-dollar divorce" was more than a legal battle; it was a deeply personal rupture that left emotional and financial scars. Looking back, Jocelyn might see this period as both a nadir and a moment of profound growth. The divorce forced her to confront the fragility of the life she had built and to find strength in herself amid the fallout.

In later years, Jocelyn faced financial difficulties that contrasted sharply with her earlier life of luxury. While these challenges might have seemed insurmountable, they also provided her with an opportunity to redefine her priorities and embrace a simpler, quieter existence. Reflecting on this chapter, Jocelyn may take pride in her ability to adapt, proving that resilience is not only about enduring adversity but also about finding purpose and joy in new circumstances.

Jocelyn's reflections on her legacy would undoubtedly be complex. She has been celebrated, ridiculed, and misunderstood in equal measure. To some, she is a symbol of excess and the dangers of vanity; to others, she represents the courage to live authentically and defy societal expectations. Jocelyn's life challenges conventional narratives about beauty, wealth, and success, forcing us to question the standards by which we judge others.

Her legacy also extends to broader cultural conversations about body autonomy and self-expression. By unapologetically embracing her unique vision of beauty, Jocelyn has become a figure who, knowingly or unknowingly, advocates for the right to define oneself on one's own terms. In an era that increasingly values diversity and individuality, her story serves as a reminder of the importance of accepting and celebrating different forms of self-expression.

Finally, Jocelyn's reflections might highlight the enduring strength of the human spirit. Despite the challenges she has faced, from public ridicule to personal loss, she has remained true to herself. Her journey is a testament to the power of resilience and the ability to reinvent oneself, even in the face of overwhelming odds.

In contemplating her life and legacy, Jocelyn Wildenstein would likely acknowledge that her story is not one of perfection but of perseverance. It is a narrative filled with complexities and contradictions, triumphs and setbacks. Yet, it is also a story that inspires, challenges, and provokes, a legacy that will continue to resonate for years to come.

CONCLUSION

Jocelyn Wildenstein's journey through life is a vivid testament to the complexities of ambition, transformation, and resilience. Her story is not one of simple fame or notoriety but rather a multifaceted exploration of self-expression, personal agency, and the consequences of defying societal expectations.

From her early dreams of grandeur in the small Swiss town of Lausanne to her rise as a celebrated figure within the world's wealthiest circles, Jocelyn's life was defined by a relentless pursuit of reinvention. Each chapter of her life, whether marked by opulence, controversy, or heartbreak, has contributed to the intricate tapestry of her legacy.

At the core of Jocelyn's journey was a constant tension between personal desire and public scrutiny. Her bold decisions, especially the extensive cosmetic transformations that earned her the moniker "Catwoman", exemplified her willingness to pursue an idealized vision of beauty, regardless of how it might be perceived.

Despite enduring ridicule, judgment, and the invasive attention of the media, Jocelyn remained steadfast in her pursuit of authenticity. Her physical metamorphosis was not an attempt to conform to mainstream beauty standards, but rather an expression of her own inner vision and autonomy.

Her marriage to Alec Wildenstein, while offering her a life of unimaginable wealth and luxury, also served as a reminder of the fragility of even the most gilded of existences. The subsequent divorce, followed by a billion-dollar settlement, was a public spectacle that showcased not only her vulnerability but also her remarkable resilience. It was a pivotal moment in Jocelyn's life, one that forced her to confront not only the dissolution of her marriage but also the unraveling of the life she had built around it.

Financial setbacks, personal struggles, and the media's harsh judgment have not dampened Jocelyn's spirit. If anything, they have deepened her understanding of herself and her place in the world. Her quieter years, following a life of excess and exposure, reflect a woman who has come to terms with her past and focused on rebuilding her future.

Jocelyn's transformation from socialite and tabloid sensation to someone who seeks peace and simplicity in private life is a powerful reminder that reinvention is a continuous process. The lessons she has learned about survival, strength, and self-definition are a testament to the enduring power of resilience.

The story of Jocelyn Wildenstein is a story of contradictions, of a woman whose public persona was often at odds with her inner reality, yet whose choices continue to challenge and inspire. Her life speaks to the human desire for transformation, for beauty, and for the right to shape one's own narrative. Through her struggles and triumphs, Jocelyn has become an emblem of defiance in the face of criticism and a symbol of the complex intersection between beauty, identity, and autonomy.

In the end, Jocelyn's legacy is not just one of outward transformation but of inner strength. It is the story of a woman who dared to live according to her own rules, regardless of the judgment or obstacles that came her way. Her life invites us to reconsider our assumptions about beauty, self-worth, and the true cost of pursuing perfection. Her journey reminds us that the pursuit of happiness is a deeply personal one, and that the only limits we truly face are those we impose on ourselves.

Jocelyn Wildenstein's unforgettable journey is a compelling narrative of ambition, courage, and the unyielding desire to reinvent oneself. As we look back on her life, we are left with a profound understanding of the complexity of the human experience and the resilience required to live authentically in a world that often demands conformity.

Her story, filled with triumph and turmoil, remains a powerful reminder that the only true measure of success is the ability to remain true to oneself, no matter the obstacles or challenges that lie ahead.

Made in United States
Troutdale, OR
02/20/2025

29146981R00169